THE SELF-LOATHING PROJECT

Women provide a glimpse into the silent epidemic of self-judgment

KATHERINE COBB

ALSO BY KATHERINE COBB

FICTION
Skyline Higher
Fifty, Four Ways

NONFICTION
Panhandle Portraits, a Glimpse at the Diverse
Residents of West Virginia's Eastern Panhandle,
Volumes 1 & 2

It Is What It Is, A Sampling of
My Favorite Columns

Published 2019
Printed in the USA
ISBN: 9781687188830

Bandito Publishing, LLC
P.O. Box 166
Farmville, VA 23901

BANDITO PUBLISHING, LLC

"The word 'Imperfect' actually spells 'I'm perfect'
because everyone is perfect in their own imperfect ways."
[ANONYMOUS]

"Owning our story and loving ourselves through that
process is the bravest thing that we'll ever do."
[BRENÉ BROWN]

"You yourself, as much as anybody in the entire universe,
deserve your love and affection."
[BUDDHA]

"It's not who you are that holds you back,
it's who you think you're not."
[DENIS WAITLEY]

Introduction

I spent a good many years wrapped up a cloak of self-loathing. Somewhere after (during?) my tenuous adolescence, I started a dialogue with myself that I didn't even notice until my late thirties. You can bet I would remember if someone else had been saying a barrage of hurtful things to me day after day, but in this case, *I was the abuser* and didn't hear these ongoing inner ramblings.

You'll read the words of many other women who share this journey. Our stories may be different, but the self-loathing is the same—a damaging, unrelenting dimmer of the precious light we all have shining inside of us.

When I identified this critical inner voice and noticed it hung out with me all day, every day, I soon realized I wasn't alone. Many women were vocal about the things they didn't like about themselves. Initially, I talked to other women about their self-loathing, then escalated to actual interviews to get them thinking about the topic more seriously. I hoped it would help me unravel this mystery, or at the very least, shine a light on it as a significant and rampant issue. I knew I'd stumbled onto something big—epidemic even (an emotional or mental plague of sorts)—except most were hiding their true feelings, or in my case, not even aware of them on a visceral level.

Through this process, my recovery began. While arduous, it was well worth the effort. First, the voice was now exposed, meaning I could argue with it, combat it, challenge it. The brain is an amazing place, and it's true you can create new pathways to change habits and thoughts. Little by little, I made solid headway. But I also fell back into deep holes many times, unsure how to pull myself out again. Habits are tough to break, and negative self-talk patiently waits, always lurking, ready to let you know how it *really is*, like a critical friend you should have disengaged from long before.

Through my research and own experience, I learned some of self-loathing is hormonal, chemical and social. Hormones wreak havoc with our thoughts and emotions, heightening responses and sometimes making us irrational. For me personally, menopause skewed my perspective even further, and moods and emotions went haywire. Or if I ate a pint of ice cream (*or a quart, but who's counting?*), I could kiss rationality and peace goodbye and usher in despair and loathing. Societal perspectives—meaning our families, peers and The Media (don't even get me started on *social media*)—also defined us and created a palpable feeling of lack and not measuring up. Finally, I realized appearance is all about perception, not reality. Skinny women loathe their bodies every bit as much as overweight women. Not everyone hates their weight, either, as the women sharing in the pages of this book will attest. Some hate a particular body part, personality trait, behavior or status. Some have a long list.

I learned in my late twenties the hardest parts of myself to see were those I'd lugged around the longest. At the root of my belief system sat the insidious goal of perfection. Self-loathing is a byproduct of that belief system. *If I berate myself enough, perhaps it will create perfect behavior.* We all know perfectionism is irrelevant, because we'll never attain it. And what does it matter? My brokenness and imperfections make me who I am and the way I am, and that, in and of itself, is pretty spectacular!

I appreciate and admire the women who participated in my research by telling their truths, secrets and stories. Some wanted to take part but were too afraid, embarrassed or unwilling to confront the pain of delving into their inner selves. No judgment here— I get it. As the responses to my interview questions trickled in, they moved me to tears. I formatted the most compelling into the essays you're about to read.

I attempted to put this information into book form over the years, but hit some roadblocks. I started the process fifteen years ago, so I'm delighted it's seeing the light of day now. I am also heartened by the volume of good messages permeating the world regarding this topic today. Women are championing self-acceptance and realizing how damaging (and false) media and advertising practices can be. They are challenging stereotypes and speaking up for injustices. We hear now about embracing ourselves, fat-shaming and being healthy at any size. We've learned about, and exposed, the diet and beauty industries. My mind boggled as I researched the mass of Instagram pages devoted to body positivity, anti-dieting and loving yourself. That's not to say there aren't just as many, if not more, still touting some diet (or a diet disguised in the more politically correct term of *lifestyle*) as well as pages devoted to uniting and perpetrate the eating disordered, those who self-harm, women who want to look younger and on and on ad infinitum. Magazine ads and stores are still filled with products to "fix" us, and make us younger, tanner, smoother, skinnier.

And while women are experiencing the biggest revolution I've seen in my adult lifetime (long overdue!), it's also clear how far we *haven't* come. So I offer this book as a token of honesty and awareness. Read their words, feel their truths, hear their pain and see if it changes how you see yourself, or want to.

I love the beauty of women just as they are. Not their exteriors, but the stuff they are made of—their toughness, their capacity for love, their willingness, their exquisiteness. My wish is that each woman could see, acknowldege and own her beauty for herself. Every day is a new day, and we can choose what we do with it. I've learned I don't have to go into the darkness or stay there if I do—and it's a rare day I experience any self-loathing (see What Helped Me on page 143 for more specifics). Recovery is doable. There are tools to climb out. Are you coming? Let me give you a hand, and we'll do it together—one day at a time, one minute at a time, one thought at a time. It's a beginning. It's *your* beginning.

How do I know you can? Because, girl, *you are limitless!*

—Katherine Cobb

P.S. If you want to see the interview questions, they're on page 137. If you want to participate in The Self-Loathing Project, you can visit my website at www.katherinecobb.com, request the questions and send your answers back to me. I will post selected stories on my website and social sites to share with others. Or, answer them for your own personal growth and discovery on your own time. Either way, *go you!*

P.S.S. I am also starting Part Two of this project—the male rendition—because females aren't the only sex to self-loathe. *Won't that be refreshing and interesting to read about?* If you are a male interested in participating, please visit my website for more information.

Perfect

How women responded to the question:
"How do you feel when I say you are perfect the way you are?"

"Like looking down at the floor and crying."

"I hope you are seeing me as a whole person and not just referring to the shell I live in. Even so, I know you couldn't possibly know about all of my imperfections."

"Take another look!"

"That's great and my husband says that, too, but it's how I feel that matters."

"Well, I could lose a few pounds."

"I think you have reached a level of growth, health and self-love that allows you to see I am perfect the way I am. Actually, *perfect* may not be the term I would use since I see perfect as the way I'll be the day I die—after I have completed my personal spiritual trail."

"For the first time in my life, I could actually believe that."

"I think you're just being sweet."

"Then you don't really know me..."

"I feel other people always see us differently than we see ourselves and we are our own worst critics."

"I am; we all are."

"Difficult to accept, but I do believe someone out there thinks that about me, whether it be my fiance, mom or friends."

"Define perfect...or do you really mean you accept me for what I am? I think that would be more appropriate. God help us if there's someone out there with no warts."

"Easy for you to say!"

"I feel you are just being nice and if you really knew me, you would see the flaws."

"Hmm...I have no cognitive framework in which to put such a statement."

"I think you are sweet but simply *cannot* accept that statement."

"I'm sure I can be self-deprecating and point out something that's bothering me at any given moment. But that's the way we're trained."

"I think you may need a shovel."

"You sound like my mom."

"I think there is something to loving myself how I am and feeling appreciated by others for it, but medical research out there says that's not true. That I might not be as healthy as possible, and therefore, I'm imperfect. Plus, I didn't get a 1,600 on the Graduate Record Examinations and was just turned down by a graduate school for a fellowship I applied for. I guess I'm fine, but fine is hardly perfect. Besides, perfect is rather boring."

"Can't possibly be. My initial reaction is to dismiss you."

"I believe you."

"I like the idea, and I would find it far easier to believe about others than about myself."

"Inner feelings are hard to share. I would think you were trying to be kind to me."

"Part of me just says thank you. Part of me still says, *yeah, right.* I know I'm perfectly made, but I'm not necessarily perfect right at the moment. The weight I carry around creates some real physical issues. But that has less to do with my being perfect in my heart and more of something I need to work on."

"I think you're trying to be supportive. I'm grateful for the journey that brought me to this place in time, but I'm looking forward to the person I will become during the remainder of the trip."

"I totally agree."

"Yeah, right! Even though people tell me that all the time, I don't believe them."

"I think you are right as far as the way my face and hair are and the way I appear in clothes, but I would say back to you as I do to others, *Well, you haven't seen me naked.*"

"I feel it is not true and brush it away."

"Everyone in this world is endowed with something special, but no one is perfect."

"It makes me feel good, and I do agree. But some things I can fix with a little workout. It boosts my confidence."

"I want to believe you, but really don't."

"Today, I can accept that, but if you had asked me the same question years ago, I would have said something different."

"I feel fine because ultimately I am happy the way I am, but sometimes it causes conflict. I guess if I were that unhappy, I would work harder to fix it, huh?"

"That makes me feel pretty and more at ease, but I still think what I think about myself."

"I think you are just being nice."

"I think that is a trite statement."

"I'll agree with you in my mind, and think it's the mindset I should carry with me for the rest of my life. But then I'll make sure I do crunches at night and only eat low-fat ice cream—just in case."

"I feel totally uninterested in hearing it."

"You may think I am perfect, but if I do not think so, then it does not matter."

"A part of me realizes this, but it is hard to really believe."

"It would be wonderful to actually feel that way, but I am far from perfect. As hard as I might try, I don't believe I will ever be in the near-perfect category."

"I feel grateful."

"I'd say, "Oh, you are sweet," but deep down I'd wish it were true. Right now, I'm okay with not being perfect…most days."

"Happy, but then I immediately scoff at that, thinking, "Yeah right. No I'm not.""

"If you mean you like me just the way I am, then I'm flattered. I am gloriously flawed and like a pair of deliciously well-worn comfy jeans; I have character and value just the way I am."

"I know it's not possible."

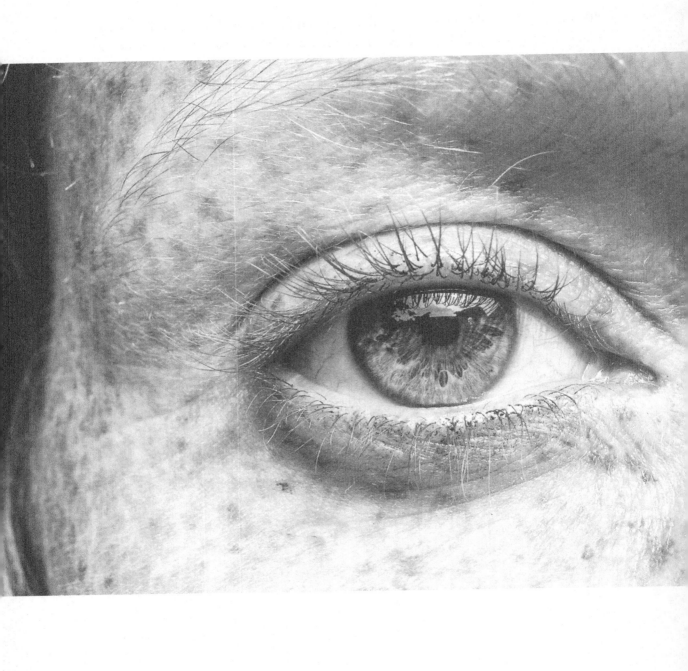

Freckled

I have spent much of my life thinking I wasn't smart enough and feeling I didn't have a perfect body. In my efforts to overcome these feelings—or fix myself—I studied incessantly, overworked myself in various jobs, over-exercised, under-ate, refused to go out because I wasn't happy with myself, and punished myself for taking off a day from work by working more than necessary the following days. *And this is just the tip of the iceberg.*

If I could resolve these feelings, I would free myself of my unattainable expectations and my life would be a nicer place. My head is constantly chattering away as to what I should be doing, how I should be nicer, better, kinder, work harder, make more money, take care of family, etc. I'd love for that to stop. If it did, I would likely sleep better, stop having such violent dreams, and feel more rested instead of exhausted after nine hours of sleep. I wake up every morning drenched in sweat and with chest pains from contorting my body so tightly. It would also do wonders for my depression, which presently is managed by medicine. I am working on this in therapy because I want to be free of my own demons. I want to be okay—to have a family and lose sleep because I spent the night staring at my little pumpkin, amazed at what I have and not because of too many other trivial things on my mind.

I have carried these feelings since fourth grade. I was the smartest kid in my class and the teacher loved me (I was a pretty nice kid), but I wanted to win the math contest, not just the spelling bees. I had a hard time accepting that Paul Ilnitski was better in math than I was. It should sound psychopathic that I remember all this. It's just nuts! I remember not liking the freckles on my body because I had family members tell me how ugly they were, so I used to cover up at the YMCA and be afraid to socialize because of my *deformities.* I refused to wear backless shirts, and shirts with no sleeves, and didn't smile in any pictures on a family vacation when I was a kid because I was so upset about showing my freckles. My pain was memorialized in these pictures, and I get so sad every time I see them. What the hell makes me so self-critical and unforgiving of a damned freckle? And this plagued me all the way through college. Can you imagine? Although family members weren't nice about it, this should have not been such a big deal, but my personality was hypersensitive to criticism. I will not do this to my children!

In addition to my upbringing, and my family being a contributing factor to these feelings, I really think I did this to myself, and I'm trying to understand why or who I wanted to impress so desperately. My parents, grandmother and sister were always supportive of what I did as well as my successes, whether it was with music, school or sports, etc. No one ever told me I didn't do well enough or I should have tried harder. This is why it's so difficult to understand where the self-loathing comes from. Although I don't know, I'm working hard to stop this ugly problem.

I'm not alone, that's for sure. *I don't know one woman who really loves who she is, and it scares me.* There are levels of self-confidence and in a lot of ways, I *am* confident. I'm a nice person. I like to help people (but there is a distorted *super helper of all* wish going on here, too). And generally, I am kind. I know I'm loved by my friends and family, but it's not always easy for me to accept. My bottom line is I'm not sure any woman is truly free of the feeling they don't need to fix themselves. From a body-image perspective, we get zero help from ads touting anorexic women as beautiful. I just wrote a letter to Tommy Hilfiger regarding his ads because there was a picture of a man and woman at a train station that was just disgusting. She was probably six-foot-three and her legs had no muscle tone and looked like arms. It made me sick and sad at the same time. The good news is I really don't want to look like her, but this has taken me years to realize. I think our society still perpetuates a crazy image of what you should look like in order to be "pretty."

I do believe someone out there thinks I am perfect, whether it be my fiance, mom or friends. It's never really about anyone else; it's more about how I think of myself. I like some things and really dislike others. I'm trying to work on not fretting about the physical level and getting to like who I am and how I relate to others. It's working, but it's a slow process.

Do I think we should all accept ourselves the way we are rather than trying to become something else? To that, I say, *Amen!* Seriously, this self-beating concept is huge and affects so many of us. I've had conversations with two women at work, both in their twenties, physically attractive, smart and outgoing, and they fight the same battle every day. I want to help them, but right now, all I can tell them is I understand exactly what they are going through and it's worth getting help because it ruins your life.

Right now, each day, to practice something positive, I could make sure I think of one good moment, conversation or action that happened as a result of me. A little pat on the back, but just for my own happiness, to remind me what makes me so special.

I'm also getting help spiritually by reminding myself that God loves me and He doesn't want me to hate myself. He wants me to grow in His love and do the best I can. I struggle with this too, because if I'm not giving up all my money, time and energy to helping others, I'm not good enough for God or I'm not good enough in general, and I am disappointing Him. Who taught me that? I think the Catholic Church, but I don't want to blame—I want to make sure I come out the other end understanding (or trying to understand) this concept is just wrong...that you can try your hardest every day and we still fail because we must. We are human. God knows it as He created us. But you have to try. It's not an excuse to be a rotten SOB. I need to believe in my heart that He loves me anyway and knows I am trying in a healthy way, which is the trick for me.

—Jane, 35

Pork Nose

I have always loathed my nose and overall body appearance, especially my breasts, which I've hated since they started to develop at age eleven. I have spent a lot of time hating these things or trying to fix them. I think if I could fix my breasts, I'd be happier and my self-esteem would greatly improve.

I'm not sure why I feel this way. In my youth, I was often told, "So and so is prettier than you are, Mary Lou." Being told you are stupid can breed self-contempt. After a while, you start believing it. I also seemed to have picked men—or maybe they picked me—that spent a great deal of time telling me I wasn't good enough, pretty enough or smart enough, and that no man would ever want a woman with stretch marks, sagging breasts, etc. The first time a classmate called me pork nose, that did it. *I can't laugh now without covering my nose so people won't see how it spreads when I laugh.*

I think most women have some sort of self-loathing. I've known beautiful women who said they felt fat, needed a facelift or some other thing that no one else believes needs *fixing*. I wish I could accept that I'm okay the way I am. I really don't know how I can move toward that kind of acceptance, except to take the best care of myself possible.

The way I feel has really kept me in a prison within myself. It has affected everything I have done in my life such as relationships (big time) and always feeling I'm not good enough. Even down to applying for jobs or being at interviews. I sit there feeling like I don't belong, as if I'm not good enough for the job. I have these thoughts even going to the grocery store, as funny as that may sound. I have caught myself thinking, *If these people knew what I looked like under these clothes, they would run in the other direction.* I have never shared these thoughts with anyone else before, and I'm fifty-five years old.

—Mary, 55

Doubt and Fear

I loathe my lack of self-confidence to pursue my dreams and goals. I'm not sure if it's fear of failure or fear of success that keeps me from taking that last big step into the unknown. I don't spend as much time as I used to thinking about this. I have a lot less time for reflection now.

It's hard to envision my life without fear and what it would be like to be brimming with confidence. My experience has proven when I take that final leap, I am rewarded with incredible blessings. However, each time, I procrastinated for long periods of time, slowly moving through the fear before I could trust my instincts and make the leap.

I saw a wonderful quote I thought I should adopt as my mantra for the next year. It was something about if you knew you could not fail, what would you attempt to do? I'm trying to stay in tune with my intuition and open to the signs as I explore different paths. At the same time, I'm filled with apprehension of choosing the wrong path, maybe the one of least resistance rather than the one requiring more faith, and therefore, more rewards.

I started hating this part of myself when I was eighteen and didn't go off to college with my friends. I enrolled at the community college instead. It may have been that my parents couldn't afford to send me to school that year, but I remember overhearing my mom tell a friend she thought I wasn't mature enough to handle college. I decided on a major in my junior year of high school and was so excited. I applied at my mentor's college and got accepted. But then I didn't go *(couldn't go?)* and it marked the first time I reached for a big goal and failed.

In terms of my upbringing, I think there were low expectations for me. Not for all of us, because my parents saw potential for each of their kids in some way. Maybe they weren't sure how to encourage my gifts.

The main thing is I don't have the academic credentials to back up my so-called talents. Isn't it funny after working twenty years in the business world and having trained other people, sometimes kids right out of college and sometimes new bosses, I still feel intimidated to write a resume that would herald my real talents and expertise? Maybe I'm just scared someone might offer me a job that meets my qualifications and I'd have to take full responsibility.

For years I described my perfect job as being someone's "right hand," i.e., the person capable of providing counsel and insight to a top executive, aid in creating corporate vision and culture and its far-reaching ramifications, and designing streamlined operations. *How wonderful of me to stay in the background.* I wonder what makes me so afraid of being the one in front—the responsibility or the success?

Women are capable of great things. I keep thinking of all the incredibly talented women I know. When I thought about what I could do for a job after my husband passed away, I kept coming back to the idea that if I could somehow create something with this group of women, we'd be so successful. They had so much energy and talent just looking for a creative outlet. If we could have found a way to harness our gifts into a cohesive business that built on our innate desire to help and support one another, it would have been incredible. But I didn't pursue it.

Accepting ourselves the way we are rather than trying to become something else is a big chicken-and-egg statement. *Where we were creates who we are.* We can't change the past without changing where we are now. When I look back at my life in snapshots, there are some of me I like better than others. Some I find laughable, others make me cry, but I'm glad I've been all of them.

One way to show myself love is to look at myself through the eyes of those that love me. There is nothing more freeing, joyous or life-affirming than looking into the eyes of someone you love and seeing love reflected back to you. With all my faults laid bare, it was always incredible to me how my husband could look at me and only see what I was capable of, and that no barrier or stumbling block was too large for me to overcome.

—Kate, 43

All the Rage

Oh, what haven't I loathed? The most significant are my temper, weight, bossiness, the need to have an answer, overall loudness and the desire to be the center of attention. Currently my anger has been causing me a constant stream of embarrassment, yet I have not been willing to change it.

From my earliest memories, my mother demanded I learn to control my temper. I distinctly remember thinking, *But how? If I could, I would.* My temper has served me well. As I have grown and matured, I have disguised my temper into more socially acceptable outbursts. However, it still scares those around me, and I still try to avoid responsibility by saying I can't control it. The truth is, I'm a scared little girl trying to get my own way in order to feel good enough.

Sometimes my anger does not rear its ugly head, and I don't remember that I have a problem with it. I am able to get along well with others and willing to accept things as they are. Other times, every little thing bothers me. I blow up and scold someone for an incidental infraction. After two or three flare-ups in a row, my whole attitude changes. I become extremely sensitive, believing nothing I do is worthwhile and questioning why on earth I have any friends or loved ones. I cannot imagine how anyone can stand being around me. The more I hate myself, the more I try to control everything around me— and how I try to control things is by scaring others more than they scare me.

If I could get rid of or fix this part of myself, I think my painful past would become more apparent. As I continue to not control others with my anger, I would have to feel the pain of abandonment (I am adopted). Intellectually, I understand fear cannot hurt me, but I continue to react instinctually and run from my fear and pain. Ultimately, perhaps I would heal and grow up. The reason I believe this is I have improved tremendously. I have healed spiritually, so I believe it will do nothing but get better. The problem is when I regress back to the fearful anger, I spiral down instead of having hope and remembering what has happened when I have trusted others, asked for help and been patient enough to allow healing to occur.

My memory of when I started hating this part of myself goes back, like I said, to when my mother told me to control my temper, and I didn't know how. I threw a chair at a boy in first grade and cracked his head. I don't remember what caused me to throw the chair, but I think I was being teased. Everyone was very disappointed in me, and I felt judged. I didn't mean to hurt the boy, but no one seemed to understand when I was in a rage, I lost the ability to rationally think through my actions. Since my family and teachers believed my rage was bad, so did I. No one knew to look at the roots—to try to see what was causing the rage. As time went on, I learned to manage the rage rather than try to heal it.

I believe my anger stems from abandonment issues. When I was growing up, I was supposed to be grateful my parents adopted me and gave me a better life, and I didn't understand why I wasn't grateful. I was angry for deep issues that remained ignored. The more I tried to control my anger, the worse it got. I felt inadequate and unwanted, and when I displayed my temper, I became unwanted. *I fulfilled my greatest fear by being so angry.* My parents adored my brother and both vied for his attention. My mother and brother had the typical mother/son relationship, but my father was so scared of women, we did not enjoy a typical father/daughter dynamic. He tried to live vicariously through my brother, who was smart, tall, dark, handsome, athletic and funny—what's not to love? I was skinny, redheaded, wore glasses and got angry—what was lovable? At least that's what I was told. The kids at school were embarrassed to be my friend. I was lonely. I falsely believed if I was popular, then everything would be okay. The only way I thought I could become popular was to become perfect. *I still feel in order to compensate for my temper, I need to be perfect.*

I see pain in most people, but I often believe my plight is worse. I envy other people who seem to hold their emotions close to the vest. I wish I could be like them. Sometimes I feel alone in thinking the way I do, but when I am honest with others, I find people feel as I do—not many about anger, but most about something within themselves they don't like. Anger is a socially unacceptable flaw to have, and many people don't have any compassion for me. When I am angry and others tell me I should control it, I feel alone and horrible. *At those times, I want to die.*

When I am still scaring people, I'm clearly not perfect. On one level, I understand God made me perfectly, and what I need to change is my actions. That is easier said than done. Many people don't understand controlling my anger is the same as controlling overeating. Just as overeaters must eat, I will get angry. The trick is to express my anger in an appropriate fashion. *Hello! Would if I could!* The problem, as I see it, is I have learned anger as a survival skill and am not completely convinced a life lived by controlling others with anger is not the best life. Now that is on a purely instinctual level. Intellectually, I understand that a life lived at the expense of others' safety is not the life I want.

Without my passion, I would lose many of my strengths, so for me to be free of my temper would mean the loss of much of my passion. This is not to say passion and anger are the same, but for me, the strong reactions I have contribute to both my passion and anger. What I want is to stop scaring people with my anger, but I don't know if I can and not give up my ability to motivate people and encourage. It's who I am.

My new commitment is to not buy into the lie I can't do anything about my anger. My experience has taught me when I connect spiritually and take responsibility for my actions, I can change anything I want. The key has been honestly understanding whether or not I want to change. When I want to change, not just when I *say* I want to change, I have grown in ways beyond my wildest dreams. However, the only ways I have been able to change deep-seated flaws is spiritually.

The best way for me to show myself love is to love others. I am able to find compassion for myself when I show compassion for others. I know that it sounds trite, but my experience has shown me when I think about and work on my flaws, they only grow. By myself I am unable to heal, but on a spiritual plane, I have healed and believe in my heart of hearts I will continue to heal.

—Julie, 45

Unfixable

There's very little I don't loathe. Pimples and wrinkles. Thighs. Nose. Weight. Stretch marks on butt and hips dating back to puberty. Hands. Nails. Teeth. Breasts. *I rarely see another woman whose appearance I do not prefer to mine.*

I spend a lot of time both self-loathing and trying to fix what I hate, like picking at pimples (which I once used to do for hours on end), pricing plastic surgery and orthodonture, coloring my hair, starving myself, forcing myself to throw-up after eating, and overspending on clothing and cosmetics I think will fix the problems.

If I could get rid of these issues or fix them, I'd just focus on another flaw. I would never be satisfied. If my legs were thin enough, I'd still be bowlegged. If my nose was perfect, my face wouldn't live up to it. But I do feel better and more in control when I have successfully "fixed" something, like when I lost weight, my skin cleared up, I found the right hair color, I grew my hair, and I wore the right clothes. This improvement in my mood is transient, but not inconsequential, so it's tempting to pursue further changes just for the mood boost. On some level, I confuse taking care of myself (eating well, exercising) with "fixing flaws" (coloring hair, buying clothes or losing weight by starvation). Both give me the same satisfaction, which makes it harder to distinguish the unhealthy impulses from the healthy ones.

From adolescence on, I would pick at my skin and then hide myself from others. I had no relationships. I refused to see friends. When I was able to overcome the compulsion, I really did have less fear of social situations. Isolation had become a habit, but it was easier for me to keep social engagements I'd made. Making my nose more symmetrical, for instance, might please me in the short run but would probably have little effect on my life. Did my skin affect me more because I felt I had made myself ugly? Don't women feel we've made ourselves inadequate when we gain weight? *Is that why we find it so distressing?*

I recall my hair darkening from white-blonde to brown between my second and third years, and I remember thinking I no longer looked like myself. I felt I'd been pretty and had lost that. *By the time I was four, I had become quite self-conscious.* I stood outside myself and judged my words, behavior and appearance. I referred to myself in the third person in the stories I told myself, including that "she" did not look like me. I found my own appearance wanting. At this time, I didn't quite experience hatred of my body, although I was certain I was not pretty and other children were. I was happy enough in my first school, where I was popular and confident, and perhaps even rather enjoyed some aspects of envying other girls. I could imagine attaining their perfection by making a few pleasant changes—getting better clothes, changing my hair—goals of which I could happily daydream. But as I was moved from school to school to school, I became awkward and anxious.

When major depression hit me at puberty, I was so self-conscious, I could hardly bear to go out at all, and I focused all my feelings of vulnerability and inadequacy on my physical self. A few years later, I was trapped in a boarding school where no hiding place was available, and there my depression and sense of myself as hideous both became overwhelming.

My progressive mother dressed me in overalls so I could play in the mud and kept my hair short. But I thought if I looked more like my next door neighbor, Donna, a little girl with long blonde hair and girly dresses whose father came to visit every other weekend, my divorced father would come to see me. But I never saw him, then or later. I thought I just wasn't pretty enough for him. Only when I was in my twenties did I learn that my mother had fought tooth and nail to prevent him from having visitation rights.

I know perfectionism and feelings of inadequacy are opposite sides of the same coin—my need to be perfect in one area arises from my sense of utter and total worthlessness in other areas. It's much worse for me to have a pimple, because I'm a complete nothing who had only clear skin to offer to start with. I'm a failure unless my book is the best, because it took me so long to write it, etc.

So why don't I think I'm good enough? Lack of reinforcement from father and peers (the latter because of the many moves)? Depression? The habit of comparing myself with others (my inside to their outsides, of course)? A habit of comparing myself to impossibly perfect fictional characters created mainly by men (I read voraciously from the age of three and always had to be forced to leave my book and go outside to play)? Childish misbehaviors for which I was excessively shamed? Two incidents of fairly mild childhood sexual abuse (well-discussed with therapists)? I don't know. None of it feels quite right. Clearly, the depression made it worse. But years before the depression began, I recall being a talkative, excitable six-year-old in a school uniform, a teacher's pet and a little bossy but with many friends, thinking about how unpretty I was. *Why?*

I'd still prefer to look like almost anyone else. In one sense, I do feel this way. But I now know other women have similar feelings, although perhaps not of the same intensity. I do feel somewhat alone in the depth and nature of my loathing for my appearance. It seems many women's dissatisfaction is limited to the issue of weight, usually weight gained in adulthood. I envy these women this focus, because I *know* I would still be unattractive even if I reached my ideal weight.

Accepting ourselves the way we are is the ideal. And I think many of us know this, but we find it difficult to internalize. I can believe this abstractly, but never when I look in a mirror. Sometimes I actually like the way I look, when I'm properly made up and dressed. *But my liking is always conditional. And it's never love.* What could I do each day to show myself love rather than participate in self-loathing? Every day? I just don't know. Emotionally, I confuse the phrases used in affirmations such as "I am beautiful" with demands I can't meet. I want to yell back, "No! I'm not beautiful!" I can go to academic treatments of the ideas about women and beauty to remind myself of their arbitrary, culturally constructed nature. Although isn't it annoying to read a feminist work like Naomi Wolf's *The Beauty Myth* and then see the author's model-perfect glamour shot on the dust jacket?

And there are a few places in our culture where I can be reminded of the beauty—the physical beauty—of all of us. Real art, not Madison Avenue fakery. I'm talking real painting, real sculpture, real dance. Enough women have written about Rubens; I'll write about my favorite choreographer, Bill T. Jones, whose "Last Supper at Uncle Tom's Cabin: The Promised Land" I saw about thirteen years ago in New York. The piece mixed dance with readings from various texts. The dancers were comprised of many amateurs, including a woman in her seventies and a man who weighed at least three hundred pounds. And at the end, in a scene of reconciliation, redemption and rediscovery of their common humanity, each member of the cast slowly, one by one, walked out naked...the seventy-year-old woman, the three-hundred-pound man and all the others. And all of them were absolutely beautiful.

—Wendy, 43

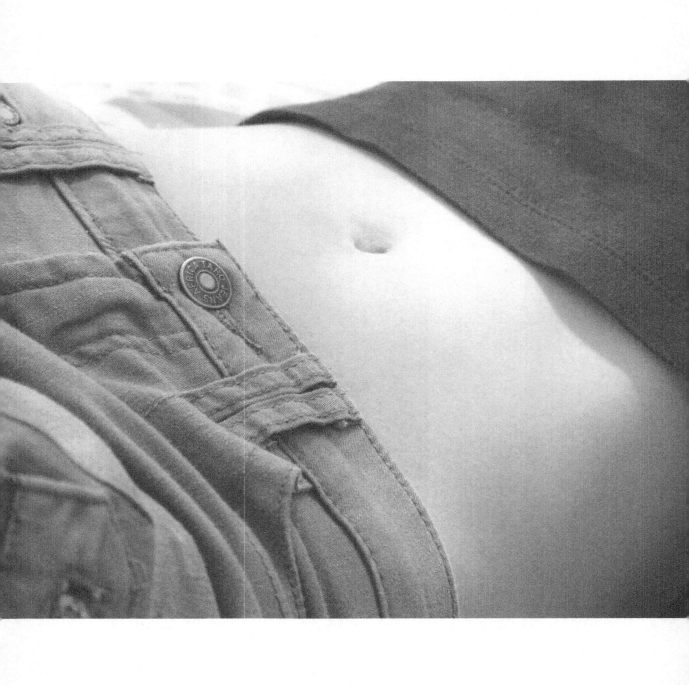

Sucking It In

I definitely have body fat issues and specifically, I loathe my belly and have since even before adolescence. I have been self-conscious about my stomach since I was eleven. I try to avoid self-loathing, but there are times that I feel so ugly and fat, I can't help it. I go to the gym a lot but rarely see any improvements. *If I had a flat stomach, I would be the most confident woman in the world.* I would flaunt it and feel attractive. I believe I would be a happier person overall.

My mother often told me to "suck it in," and so I was always aware my stomach wasn't nice to look at. I'm sure it's the American media that's helped to make me feel unattractive at times. And hearing about dieting in the media has also had an effect on me. Every ad, study or fad diet makes me feel like I never try hard enough to fix my weight problem. I also compare myself to a lot of beautiful, slim friends. I know no one's perfect, but I'm jealous of my skinny friends who don't seem to worry about their bodies. I'm not alone in my plight, though, and I get that.

It would be an amazing world full of happy people if we could all accept ourselves. I wouldn't be able to not beat myself up, at least sometimes. I wish I didn't self-loathe, but it's close to impossible in the world in which I've grown up. *I do love myself, but there will always be things about myself I will never accept as good enough.*

To show myself love, I could tell myself how lucky I am for what I have—it's a lot more than what some people have. I'm lucky I have both my legs. I'm lucky to have full hair. I am lucky I have loving friends and family who accept me for who I am.

—Lara, 24

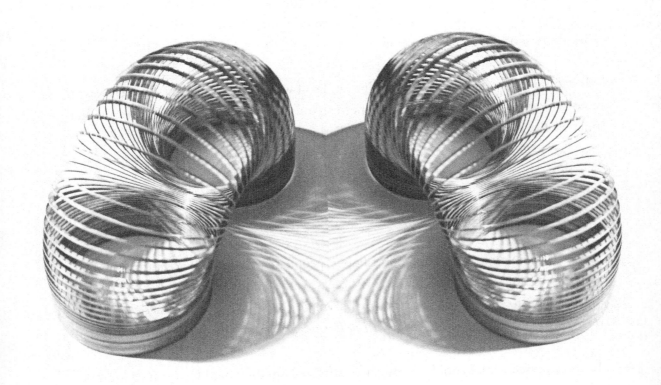

Slinky Titties

My breasts have been the target of most of my self-loathing. After that comes my sexuality, then my abundance of insecurity, and can't forget the old lack of self-esteem. When it comes to my breasts, I had problems from the very start. The first thing I ever heard about them was when a class bully in the sixth grade said I had *slinky titties*. I was mortified, and it only got worse from there. Then came the purple stretch marks that remained well into my teen years, only to fade to a light pink. When I see society's—or better yet, the media's—definition of what's beautiful in the breast department, I become painfully aware that mine look nothing like them. They are quite settled and could never even closely have been described as perky. I have hated them as long as I've had them. Sad, I know.

I'm not sure how to quantify the amount of time I've spent self-loathing because I almost feel it has been a constant. The way I used to try and fix how badly I felt about myself was to be very attention-seeking, mostly from males. As a result, I took risks with my body and health I feel a lot of shame about. I carried huge misconceptions about love versus sex, and had no ear for my inner voice. As for my breasts, I can't tell you how many times I've stood in front of a mirror and lifted the skin above them, showing myself how much better they would look if they weren't so droopy. I've commented that if I didn't plan to have children, I would save my money and get a breast lift.

I used to think I would be better and look better if only I had perkier breasts or straight, white teeth. I know now it's deeper than those concerns. If I had the perkiest of breasts, or the whitest of smiles, inevitably there would be some other target to take their place.

I've been insecure for as long as I can remember. I was shy and reserved growing up, and got picked on and bullied a lot. I was also sexually abused. Looking back on this now, as I'm active in my healing, I'm aware of the ultimate violation and subsequent confusion this brought me. I blamed myself. I never told. I felt dirty, disgusting, shameful and thoroughly confused. When someone who is supposed to love you as a child hurts you sexually, all of the sudden there's no difference between love and sex and you become so vulnerable. I hated myself and my body. I hated what grew to be my sexuality. I had no reference for what was appropriate and inappropriate.

In addition to the abuse, my mother was the daughter of abusive and neglectful alcoholic parents. She came out of that childhood quite skilled at putting on good appearances and establishing a false sense of control. My mother had a painful habit of exaggerating my accomplishments to people both in and outside of our family. I brought home B's and C's, she would brag I was a straight A student. When she lied about me or our family to someone, I was always so confused about it, wondering why she did that. When I would challenge her, she would yell at me never to contradict her. So much for the truth! I was already quite skilled in lying anyway. I believe these factors, coupled with others, paved the way for a clear route to self-hatred.

I do find I frequently compare myself to other women. Most of the time, I come out on the bottom. I think they have perfect bodies or features. They have better, brighter personalities or better senses of humor, fashion, whatever. I know I'm not alone, but I can sure fool myself into thinking I am. This has been stronger in times when I've been more isolated.

I hate to think of how much time and energy I've spent on perpetuating negative beliefs about myself, not doing the things that would bring me joy and happiness because deep down inside I've tricked myself into believing I don't deserve to be happy and healthy. More than anything in the world, I want to feel good about myself every minute of every day, because that is what I deserve. I am a worthy, wonderful human being and I deserve to grow into all of my potential. So does everyone else.

To show myself love rather than participate in self-loathing, I can acknowledge all of the gifts I've been given. I can thank the Great Spirit for this abundant earth, and all of its beautiful creatures. I can look at myself with love and acceptance. I can pay more attention to the compliments I receive from those who love and support me. I can recognize the amount of people in that crowd grows a little every day. I can make better choices about what I put in my body, who I spend my time with and what I watch and listen to in the media.

Most importantly, I want to keep talking. I find the more I share with others about my experiences and pain, the more I'm able to work through it and move forward. Sharing with others is a lifeline to my true fabulous self, and a line for the truly fabulous selves I know to open up as well. Sharing brings openness and validation. The more I talk with other women about our struggles, the less I feel alone in mine. *I have to keep talking.*

—Mindy, 27

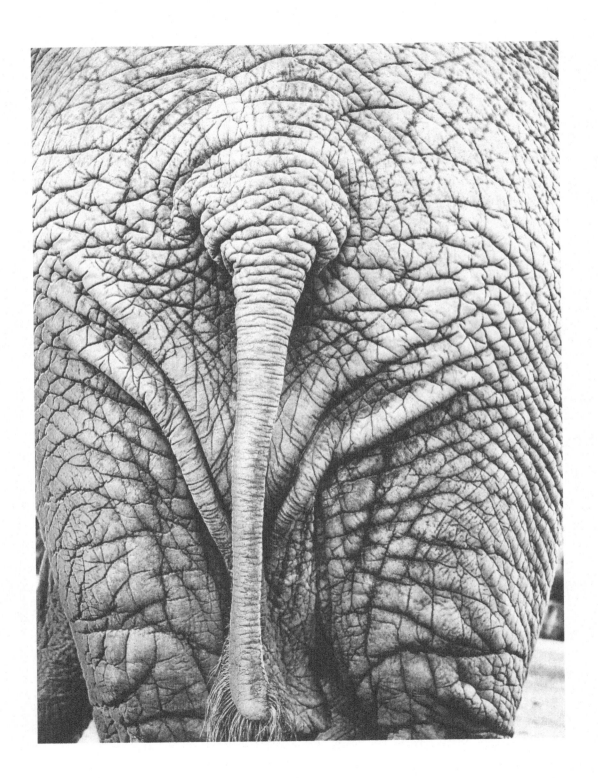

Saggy Mess

Physically, I have always had a hate relationship with my rear end and upper thighs. My rear end I refer to as my *saggy mess* while my upper thighs earn the title of *saddlebags*. From the point I stopped wearing hand-me-downs from my brother's closet, I've had a negative body image. I started hating this specific part of myself in junior high, my most vulnerable time in life. But then again, I hated everything in junior high.

To combat what I believed to be poor genetic makeup, I dieted and exercised both with and without enthusiasm and true commitment. Let's face facts: we have all been on the diet and exercise plan that allows us to treat ourselves to ice cream after a vigorous workout that includes more walking than actually being aerobic.

Through my ignorance of proper nutrition and exercise, I even attempted Nutri-System, a diet plan that included group discussion of how well or poorly one performed the prior week as well as expensive meals. I gained weight, and I hated my body.

Today, though I am more educated on proper nutrition and exercise regularly, I am still disappointed with the way I look. Even when I was in the best shape of my life, after entering a Body For Life competition, I remained unhappy with my upper thighs and rear end. In fact, those problem areas seemed to stand out even more when the rest of my body was prime. I still work out on a regular basis, I still watch what I eat, and I still hate my saggy mess.

I think I use my negative body image as an excuse not to do a lot of things in life—and rely on that excuse. If I didn't have the excuse, it would scare me because there would be nothing standing in my way. *It is almost comforting to know my saddlebags are there for me...holding me down.* I'm sure I could get used to going to the beach without a pair of baggies or wearing a skirt without worrying about the way my ass looks, but I think it would also add more pressure to maintain this newly sculpted figure. Instead of people greeting you with, "You look great!" you'll have the whispers of "She sure has put the weight back on."

Honestly, I have thought of taking the easy way out. You know...the "L" word. Lipo. What stops me other than the cost? The knowledge that I was not able to combat the saggy mess on my own and that in a small way, I would be cheating myself of an incredible accomplishment. Quite honestly, I enjoy working out. Maybe not the process of getting ready and going, but during and after, there is no greater feeling. It can be a truly amazing experience if you allow yourself to take full advantage of whatever time you can chisel out of your hectic day.

I have just visited the topic of how my upbringing may have contributed to my self-loathing and the answer is a resounding yes! Though I do not blame anyone but myself for what I feel today (I am my own master), I do think I learned to be or think certain things from my past. I know I need to reeducate or reprogram myself. Knowing is easy. Putting it to action is difficult. Growing up, I found comfort in food. I would even eat to spite people that cared about me. If they said I was fat or gaining too much weight, which they did, I would eat just to emphasize that I was the one in control. I also believe too much emphasis was placed on my looks growing up. All kids in a family dynamic have titles...the smart one, the problem one, the cute one. I was the cute one, and I hated it! I received a writing scholarship in my academic career and still the emphasis was placed on what I would wear to the ceremony. I am not innocent in the portrayal. I learned to think it was my best feature.

I pick on myself because I know myself. I am the only one that knows every little secret about myself, and I am an easy target. If I see a woman who wears something well and has the confidence to do so, I think to myself, how lucky is she. But I can also look at the same woman and know she probably has something she hates about herself. I look at women that can throw on a pair of jeans or slip into a dress and not worry about control-top pantyhose or underwear lines and wish for that same freedom. I look at women that are so skinny, yet have big boobs, and wonder how it can be physically possible. I wish my boobs weren't the first place my body loses the weight.

Self-acceptance is absolutely right, and I would wish that for everyone, but I believe loving ourselves is one of the most difficult things to give ourselves.

There is a slogan that says, "What would Jesus do?" I would apply that to myself and instead ask, "What would I do?" What would "I," acting in my highest sense of self, do in any given situation? What would "I" want for myself and what would "I" want to show of myself?

For the most part, I think women are lazy. They are not lazy in the workplace, the community or their homes, but they are lazy when it comes to themselves. *We put ourselves at the bottom of the to do list. We are our lowest priority, and it is acceptable to us and to those around us.* I think we'd all have so much more to give if we allowed ourselves to have grace in our imperfections. We're all responsible for managing our lives, and at the top of our list should be our own health, emotionally and physically. Every woman should move her body at least three times a week. Every woman should eat healthy food that helps her mind and body to function at its best. And every woman should treat herself even if she feels she may not deserve it—because in most women's minds, they never deserve it.

—Grace, 35

Enough

I spent most of my life not liking my body and face, but in recent years, I have felt more confident and attractive. I have great breasts, but until I was thirty years old, I despised them as if they were *deformed*—don't even know why now. I also spent time hating how my face looked when I smiled and thinking my nose was too wide and misshapen. Puberty is about when I started to become disappointed in my looks. I was much taller and more developed than my peers and found it difficult. My brother pointed out how I should shade the width of my nose to make it appear narrower. It hadn't occurred to me that it was too wide yet—*thanks, bro'*. He also told me if I wore skirts, my ass would look smaller. He didn't get me on the ass thing; I had already experienced positive feedback.

I don't spend much time anymore on the things I can't control, but I am always on or breaking a diet, and I am still very dissatisfied with my size. If I could fix being too thick, I would feel better, but I need to feel better so being thick is not serving as a distraction from the underlying issues. *I believe self-loathing the external is a manifestation of self-loathing the internal.* It provides a distraction from dealing with emotional pain, which is harder to fix than even a hundred-pound weight loss. The moments in my life when I felt my best, I also looked my best, exercised and ate well, but looking good was the result of feeling good, not the reason.

I have never known a woman who was satisfied with the way she looked and I've only known one woman who never spoke against herself. When I see a beautiful, well-maintained, very made-up woman—I call her the neon sign woman, tanned and thin with styled hair and makeup applied—I almost feel sorry for her in a loving way. Such pressure to look so done up must be exhausting. Although I still have attacks of the fat-and-uglies, I now feel *I am enough*. I am certainly more than my figure, but it took until recently to get there. Self-acceptance is key to happiness and self-love. To show myself love, I like a self-affirmation: I am good enough, smart enough and dogonnit, people like me!

—Kimberly, 36

Consumed

Not a day goes by when I don't think about what I'm eating, what I should be eating, and how I'm feeling—as in, how fat do my thighs feel? How fat does my bottom feel? I can't fathom there are people in the world that never give it a passing thought, but I've known some of these girls—beautiful, with great bodies. One of my friends said the only exercise she got was walking to 7-Eleven to get something good to eat. I can't imagine the freedom in that because I am always thinking about the things I don't like about my body.

I spend a fair amount of time on the subject—and trying to fix it. I am always trying to improve in some way, whether it's by dieting or increasing my exercise. While I have spent plenty of time self-loathing, as I approach forty, I am trying to accept myself more. I hope in letting go of some of my longing to be better or perfect, I can stop beating myself up and become free.

I know when I am at a reasonable weight, I feel better about myself, have more energy and generally feel happier. This feeling compels me to push on and stay focused on losing weight or "fixing" the problem when I am overweight. This is not to say I have a desire for plastic surgery or anything extreme—although reduced thighs and liposuction would be nice—but I do like to feel the best I can about myself and that seems to include, in a big way, the number on the scale.

I have worried about my body and its imperfections as long as I can remember. Most of my family is pretty small. My mother was a mere ninety-eight pounds when she married. I will never be that small, so there certainly seemed to be expectations I could not meet. Also, I was the third girl and heard over and over, "*You're* the baby sister?" The implication was, "How could that be? You are so much bigger than your sisters." I think this contributed in a tangible way to viewing my size and imperfections as real problems. I also tend to be a bit of a perfectionist, so that doesn't help, either.

Society in general is consumed with people's outward appearance. This influences girls, and women, a great deal.

We all have shortcomings. Some are visible and some are not, but everyone has something. I can't imagine not having to think about "fixing" yourself, in terms of the physical. To some degree, I sometimes feel alone—though in going to the gym and doing weight-loss programs, I'm aware I'm not.

I agree we should all accept ourselves the way we are, but how do we get there? I could try to be less obsessed with my weight and focus more on being healthy and thankful for good health. I have often said if I spent as much time doing a healthy activity as I did obsessing about what I have eaten or what my thighs look like, I could be in great shape. Stop thinking and just do. Be gentle with myself and work toward self-acceptance.

—Carolyn, 39

Hourglass Figure

Having been told in my youth that I had an hourglass figure—with all the sand at the bottom—my hips and butt are one spot I loathe. Also being teased about my mosquito-bite breasts—that if I scratched them they might get bigger—is another. I definitely started my self-loathing as a teen.

When I was younger and still aspiring to the hourglass figures of teen and fashion magazines, I was pretty obsessed with myself. I remember reading my breasts were *large enough* if I could hold a pencil underneath them. I went through all kinds of contortions in front of my adolescent mirror trying to figure out how to hold that pencil! Another message: when you stood with your legs together, there should be a space between your ankles and calves, calves and knees and knees and hips. While I tried to console myself that two out of three wasn't bad, I still longed for those long legs and just one more space. Fortunately, pushing fifty and facing wrinkles, gray hair and other body atrocities, my priorities are shifting. As Popeye says, "I yam what I yam."

I think what complicated matters was the constant message that I wouldn't amount to anything. I wasn't recognized for being bright, funny and creative. As I've aged, I finally drowned out the not-only-are-you-fat-and-ugly-but-stupid-too thoughts. With some therapy, I now take limited credit for my talents having nothing to do with my body. But then the Swedish influence of my heritage burns through...*I certainly don't want to think too well of myself by thinking I am smart*. I got it coming and going growing up.

I've discovered losing weight or inches would not change my life. Letting go of the hurt of being teased by my father...*that* might make a difference. I tend to poke fun at myself about my lower half. I don't know what I would do if I couldn't joke around!

When I think about why I feel this way, I think about a mentor of mine who talks about the *not enoughness* ingrained in us. "You got all A's, but what happened with this B?" "You cleaned up your room, but what about those toys over there?" "You got dressed, but your shoes are on the wrong feet." I got subtle messages along with the overt ones. Even when I did something "right," it was to my father's credit..."You are a chip off the old block," rather than "You did it." Or, "I am so proud of you," rather than "You should be proud of yourself." I got very little credit for my successes. I think many women have "made it" because they are trying to prove to their ghosts they are worthy. That is my case.

Being raised as a girl child in the 1950s and 1960s was especially difficult. We spent childhoods with stay-at-home, perfect moms, being groomed to be a wife and mother and support our husbands. We entered young adulthood in the midst of women's lib with no role models. It was a difficult transition complicated by my brother's sudden death and realizing I could lose a husband that quickly and not be able to support a family. When I was graduating from college, my dad ran off with a bleached blonde and it struck me that I could give twenty-five years of my life to a man who could leave me and never look back. My mother worked in a dress shop for minimum wage in her fifties and sixties, as she had no other skills. I went immediately into graduate school to make sure the same fate would never await me.

When my brother was killed, I found out the life insurance policies for my brothers were double what they were for the girls. My parents were saving to put the boys through college, but there were no plans for my sister or me because we would marry and someone would take care of us. I wanted to be a veterinarian, but was told in 1973 by my high school guidance counselor that it wasn't fair for me to take a man's place in vet school. When I was in graduate school and going through a divorce from an abusive relationship, my mother asked what I did to make Gary so mad. She later told me if I was going to attend graduate school and have this *career*, I should probably not plan to marry and have a family since it wasn't fair to my husband. The messages run deep!

I believe there is a whole spiritual side of who we are that is undeveloped...that is truly who we are. Exploring that line of thinking has been very helpful. I also believe we have more control over our thoughts than we've been taught. Our thoughts control our feelings and there is all kinds of research that supports this. We get into ruts of thinking...neural pathways, if you will. We can change those ruts, but it has to be done consciously and with full awareness. *I can choose to be different.*

I am really dedicated to raising my own kids differently. What astonishes me is my daughter, who from the age of four has been concerned about clothes that make her *look fat*. We've had many huge to-dos about her self image. Where in the hell does a four-year-old get ideas about being fat when she has a beautiful body, exactly at the fifty percent mark for height and weight? We emphasize health rather than weight and try and limit food, especially sweets, as a reward or comfort.

I think it would be interesting to explore what we, as parents, do differently. Ironically, my son has helped me sort through all kinds of drama with my father's rage and my daughter has helped me sort through all of the body image and self-image stuff. If we don't get it the first time around, we have children who help us work through it later. Let's hear it for good therapists who help us see those patterns!

—Cheri, 48

Not Enough

When it comes to self-loathing, it's not just one thing. At one point, it was an overall feeling of, well, everything. I wasn't *good enough* in so many ways. When I was little, it was my freckles and frizzy hair. Then it was the essence of me. At eight, my mother told me I had better study hard as I had nothing else to offer. She was very good at reminding me of all the things I wasn't good at and never would be. That, combined with the fact I looked twelve until I was eighteen years old and a sophomore in college had me not really liking anything about myself. I wasn't thin enough, pretty enough or smart enough, and being poor, nothing I had was nice enough. The only thing I could control was working hard and eating less, so I did. At least then I could say, "I'm a hard worker" and "I'm doing everything I can."

I have spent the majority of my life trying to be thinner, stronger, smarter, better. Always trying to be *enough* for everyone. I actually spend a lot of time trying not to loathe how my chest looks like a sixty-year-old's, or how my stomach isn't ripped despite how hard I train and eat right, or that my muscles are too small, or that I'm not smart or organized enough. I also don't communicate well. Although my heart is big and I only try to help, people often misinterpret me as being mean. In addition, my significant others continually remind me I am still not good enough as I am, and I need to improve this, that or the other.

I spend a lot of energy combating the aforementioned and looking for the positives— places where results have proven I am good enough. That's one reason why I love racing. Every time I approach a starting line, I don't know if I will be able to do X, but I love surprising myself with what I am capable of, and it helps me stretch the possibility of what I think I can do.

I only recently found the courage to try and stop limiting myself. If only I had found that earlier, my life might be very different.

Self-loathing has kept me from *even trying* many things…sports, auditions, colleges, earning my Ph.D. If I didn't have it holding me back, I would be a successful artist, have a doctorate, probably have a great family, and maybe would have been an Olympian.

Hating the physical stuff began when I was about fourteen when someone saw me eating a Snickers bar and said, "You are going to get fat if you eat that." *One little statement started my earnest lifelong quest to educate myself on how not to get fat.* The irony is, the more I tried to get smaller, the bigger I got, and then I felt more like a failure because I always gave in and ate.

I know other women don't like things about themselves no matter how beautiful, smart or wonderful I think they are. I believe we're trained to think that. *Everything tells us from a young age we're not good enough.* Our eyelashes aren't long enough, lips aren't red enough, skin isn't perfect enough, hair isn't shiny enough, and we aren't skinny enough or curvy enough, etc.

Accepting ourselves the way we are rather than trying to become something else is what I'm working on daily. To show myself love, I can remind myself I am helping many people, which is more important than thinking of myself. No matter what I look like or what I am *not* good at, at least I am doing that.

—Laura, 36

Older, Wiser, Softer

My weight was an issue in high school, when everyone seemed to be thin. When I went to college, I became thin. I am now forty, have three kids (and I will now state for the for the record that I am neither fat nor thin) and am pretty accepting about who I am.

Although I don't waste a lot of energy thinking about it, I'd always like to lose the ever-present ten pounds. More for the way my clothes fit than anything else. Do I wonder what my twenty-something self would say if she looked in the mirror now? Hell yes! I know she'd see an older face, graying hair and a body with saggy breasts, relaxed muscle tone (doesn't that sound PC?) and what I believe is the start of a varicose vein. I know my twenty-something me would be shocked by the image in the mirror. But that's not all of who I am. I'm a mom. I'm half of a happy marriage. I've been a successful businessperson (and may be again someday). I'm healthy, insanely happy and laugh and dance around the kitchen to bad '80s music. I hope my former self would look past the image in the mirror and say, *I want to be her when I grow up.* Although my clothes would fit better if my belly was smaller, love-handles diminished and breasts were back where they once were—it wouldn't change my life. I'd still be me.

My mom and I had a lot of battles over my adolescent weight. I know she viewed me as an extension of herself. I was fat; she was a failure. What's most interesting is she had similar issues with her mom. I hope the cycle will be broken when my daughter becomes a teen.

My parents went through a divorce when I was younger. I spent my seventh to twelfth grade years watching my mom self-destruct because her fragile psyche was shattered by the belief she was not worth loving and her life was not worth living. The other portion of my adolescence was spent alone, smoking a ridiculous amount of pot, which made me fat, lazy and stupid. If I'd had parents that encouraged me, even took walks with me, it could have been different. Don't get me wrong. This is not a statement about how awful my school years were or what crappy parents I had. That's an old song—one where too many of us know all the words by heart.

Truth be told, I had fun in high school. I had great friends, which kept me sane, and other adults who stepped up to the plate to help my self-confidence. But peers are not kind in high school. I know, I know, it's hard to believe. *I once was standing behind the most popular guy in school when he pronounced that if I lost about seventy pounds, I'd be beautiful.* Ouch. Keep in mind I would have been emaciated or dead if that were true. To add insult to injury, he was a nice guy and a good friend. He was very apologetic, so at least I had that going for me. When we saw each other as adults, he mentioned that of all the girls in our circle, he was looking forward to seeing me most because he didn't have any reservations. After all, there wasn't the baggage of a failed relationship. He was right. I've never had reservations about attending my reunions. They've been great, and I've had an amazing time at each one. But did I ever dream of losing weight so that the sweet, popular boy would ask me out? Do you have to ask?

I know there are women who look better than I do and those who don't. I have a wonderful husband who has never even whispered a negative thing about my weight. I gained a lot during each of my pregnancies, and that was tough. There is nothing like looking at your naked self after a baby. Ugh! He loved me, took me to Lane Bryant and told me I was beautiful. What a guy! It made losing weight easier.

Lately, I've been frustrated about my breasts. Again, it's an issue about finding clothes and looking good in them. They seemed to grow as the years passed. Now they are where no good breasts should be. I'd love them to be up where they once were. Maybe a little smaller, too. Carrying double-Ds makes my neck hurt and my back ache sometimes.

Do I think other women have it made because they don't need to fix themselves? No. Is it easier for them to get dressed in the morning? I don't know. I do know I'm not alone when it comes to body image concerns. And I also know when I was thinner, I didn't have a better job, more money or a better life. True, I was younger and probably didn't appreciate my body the way I should have (oh, yeah, the youth thing could explain why I didn't have more money or a better job).

I'm thankful and grateful to be who I am. *I know these are the good years.* The angst of being a teen is behind me. The foolishness and self-doubt of my twenties are long gone. I'm older, wiser and softer. It's okay. There are times that I feel frumpy and tearful. Then there are times when I look in the mirror and smile. Life is good.

God, I sound so preachy, but here it goes: There's a whole world of oppressed women and we are not among them. I think white women in America are our own worst enemies. Be real. We complain about our bodies because we have the food to abuse, healthcare to ignore and a lifestyle to take for granted. I complain when my clothes don't fit the way I wish when I could just as easily be draped from head to toe in a black veil. Life is too short to not embrace who we are and just be happy. That doesn't mean that we should be complacent—*but celebrate who we've been, who we are now and who we will hopefully become.*

A few years ago I had the opportunity to go to the Congressional Black Caucus celebration. *Wow!* The women dressed in bright colors that hugged every curve of their shape. Everywhere I turned there were jewel tones, shimmering fabrics, feathers, stripes and patterns. Me? I was in a little black dress. First, let me state the obvious. There will never be a Congressional White Caucus—but if there was, it would be filled with little black dresses, most with labels showing single digits. How boring.

—Beth, 40

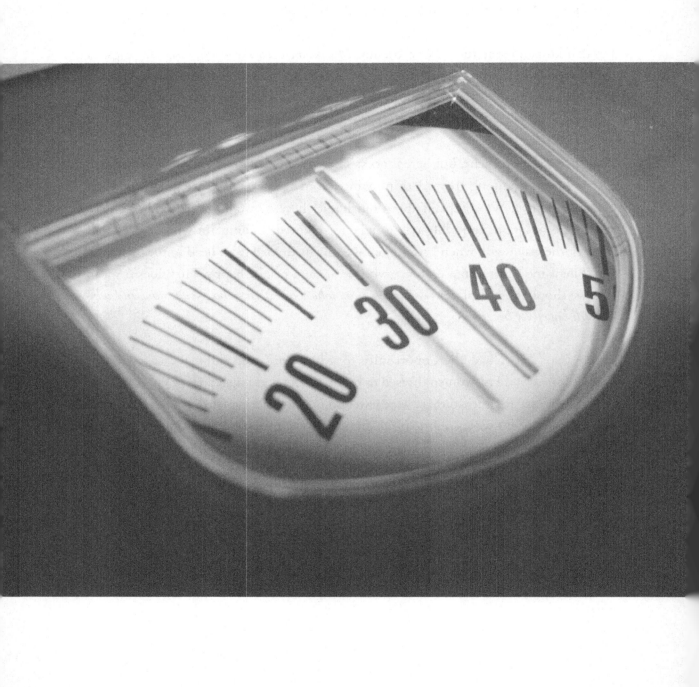

Fifteen Pounds

My weight has been an issue for me since I was sixteen—not that I was anywhere near overweight. I began dieting, and by the time I was nineteen, I had anorexia nervosa. When I married at twenty-five, my wedding dress had to be taken in more than once. I actually had to gain ten pounds so I would fit into my dress on my wedding day! My obsession hurt my relationship with my husband and then I became pregnant three months into the marriage. I gave up my dieting so I could be a healthy, pleasant wife and mother.

Today, I am the mother of three children and I am fifteen pounds overweight. Over the years, I have told myself it was worth it to give my body over to my children through pregnancy and nursing. *But I really do hate my body now.* My belly is disgusting with its stretch marks, fat and stretched-out bellybutton. I view this middle-age change in metabolism as a betrayal by my own body. If I had known at sixteen how real fat looked, I like to think I would have enjoyed my youthful, pre-mom body.

As a homeschooling parent, I get no "me" time to walk, exercise or go to a gym. I find that very frustrating! I would love to be able to concentrate on my diet and work out again. If I could fix this part of myself, I believe I would have more energy and self-confidence. *I could even let my husband see me without any clothes on!*

When I think about contributing factors to my weight issues, I can look, in part, to my upbringing. My father was sexually inappropriate with me and I felt my mother never liked me. When I was anorexic, I wanted to literally disappear into thin air. I also think the media is constantly telling me I'm not good enough. Obesity research and reports make me worry about my health. *Fifteen extra pounds equals fat and unhealthy.* I think all women are unhappy with their bodies, and it really bugs me when thin women complain about being fat!

If I could accept myself the way I am, I don't believe I'd be accepted by society, so what would be the point? Oh, and let's not forget the fact that my fifteen extra pounds are working against me, trying to kill me—or so says the latest research.

Life's responsibilities keep me too busy to dwell on this issue, so loathing may be too strong of a word today. *However, I do go to bed at night wishing I could have plastic surgery.* I guess what I'm trying to say is that, right now, I do love myself for all I do for the ones I love.

—Christin, 35

Eating Disordered but Trying

I've long struggled with body image. From the time I was eleven, I have been eating disordered. I became severely anorexic over the summer between sixth and seventh grade, but I imagine things were starting to click in my mind before that. That fall, I was sent to a therapist, a man to whom I refused to speak. I was weighed regularly and intimidated into eating by my parents (e.g., "If you don't eat that, I'll get your father"). After eleventh grade, I took a turn for the worse and lost about half of my body weight. I was checked into a hospital and once medically stable, I was transferred to an eating disorders clinic. When discharged—and still seriously underweight—I returned to school for the second half of my senior year. At this point, I felt ridiculously fat but started to tire of the constant starvation, exercise and deceit. I began to binge and then purge through exercise, laxatives and ipecac.

I don't have memories of being normal in that sense of the word. I must have been a carefree kid at some point, but my mother tells stories of how I'd obsess over first grade homework, erasing the letters I considered imperfect in form so many times, I'd rip holes in the pages.

The dynamics of my family are complicated. My father is not particularly great at showing his emotions in healthy ways and demanded nothing short of perfection from all of us (I have two siblings). One sister is fifteen months older and was a year ahead of me in school. Inevitably, comparisons arose, as we went to small schools and shared many teachers year after year. My junior year, when I came in second to the defending state champion in the cross-country district finals, my dad did not compliment me. Rather, he wanted to know why I didn't win. I went from being on cloud nine to immediately feeling defeated. I'm not sure why I cared so much about his affection and praise, other than his being my parent, but it hurt.

My mother was a blast so long as Dad wasn't around. We lived dual lives of a sort. She was very submissive to him, which was a bad message for us kids—Daddy's scary if

Mom's afraid of him. In addition, my extended family members are high achievers. They are Ivy league-educated, teach at universities and world-renowned in their specialties. This is a burden as much as a blessing at times. I am grateful for all the privileges and luxuries I enjoyed as a kid, but certainly would have liked to have a little more time to *just be me*.

I lost two friends the summer I began exhibiting anorexic symptoms—one moved across the country, the other across the state. I'd gone to a school with a strong contingent of Jewish kids and when I matriculated, lots of the kids knew each other already because they'd gone to Hebrew school together. My family was not Jewish, and I felt very left out in this bigger world.

Years of therapy taught me part of my particular issue is societal: I live in a world where thin is considered desirable, I'm surrounded by images and messages that herald thin women (and men) as the ideal, but there is certainly a personal factor as well. I would have been dysfunctional or needed an outlet for my unexpressed emotions in positive ways regardless of what body image messages I received from society. Perhaps having it as an option led me there. I could have become an alcoholic (*though I feared the calories*), drug addict, acted out sexually or done one of many other things. Instead, I took the route that seemed the most conformist or easiest to "get away with" in my particular family situation. Unless it was incredibly extreme—which in my case, it became—I escaped attention because I was a quiet kid.

Today, I consciously try not to obsess over food. I've reintroduced many of the foods that were off limits, but fatty dairy products and red meat are still taboo. *Most days are pretty good, but there are a few days each month when I count calories.* If I could get rid of or fix this part I hate, I'd have a lot more time on my hands to do positive and productive things.

I think many people obviously feel the need to fix themselves. I work at a place with a Weight Watchers group. I'm not in the group (all I need is another excuse to obsess over caloric intake, exercise and whatnot) but many of my coworkers are. Last fall was ridiculous. I couldn't grab a piece of candy from my boss's dish without seeing a handmade sign about how many points (the Weight Watchers substitute for calories) each type of food contained. People were constantly discussing food in terms of its points or how many they could have or how many they had left. It was quite aggravating to try so hard not to obsess, only to be confronted with this. You also see people who obviously feel inadequate on TV, lamenting their diets and failures, writing or calling into news programs about their weight-loss plan.

Accepting ourselves the way we are rather than trying to become something else sounds good in theory, but in practice, it's much tougher. In terms of self-love instead of self-loathe, my therapist used to suggest stuff like taking a bath, having a cup of tea or treating myself to a piece of clothing I actually thought I looked good in. I suppose I could respect myself by taking time out for healthy things (diet, exercise, rest, etc.), standing up for myself and following my conscience and dreams. It would be nice to have a piece of cake instead of banishing all sweets or eating the whole cake. I just hate how hokey it sounds to say, "I'm going to do this to show I love myself." I wish we didn't have to do this stuff so overtly, that it was just a natural part of being. I hope to be able to get close before having kids so they can grow up feeling comfortable with themselves.

—Rachel, 26

Weight a Minute

I hate my weight, particularly my hips and thighs, and have since I was a teenager. Daily, I think about ways to lose weight. I feel like if I could just overcome this *weakness,* I would be stronger, more confident and more successful.

My father loves physically beautiful women and has always made it clear overweight people disgust him. He left my mother and admits it was partly because he was no longer physically attracted to her. She gained weight after giving birth to three children. Not much weight, but some. When I became a teenager, people started paying attention to me and calling me "pretty." I was always quiet and bookish before that, but suddenly I became popular for my looks. I guess a part of me thinks people primarily, or at least initially, are drawn to me because of my physical appearance. I worry that if I cease to be "pretty," I will again become invisible. *Do I really have enough attributes, besides my looks, to attract people?*

I don't feel alone in this. I realize many women are unhappy about their weight. I greatly admire women who are big yet still radiant and happy.

My rational mind agrees with the message we should all accept ourselves, and this is the message I want to transmit to my young daughters, but I am not emotionally developed enough to live this statement daily. I'm working on it. I have stopped allowing myself to weigh in each morning and I try to revel in the positive things I have accomplished, and in my life in general.

—Wanda, 35

In the Light

At one time in my life, especially during my late teens and early twenties, I loathed different parts of my body. I have a tendency to carry weight in my midsection, and I hated it at the time. As my body developed into a woman, I attracted a tremendous amount of attention from males. This attention turned into self-destruction because I was not mentally ready for sexual attention. A downhill pattern began with my self-image and remained with me into my early twenties.

I slowly began to change my way of thinking by talking to other females with similar traits and insecurities. Then a friend handed me a book that changed my life: *Succulent Wild Woman* by Sark. This book started the spin that spun me out of that terrible place with myself.

Now, after several self-help books and much quiet time and meditation, I am learning to love all parts of myself, including my physical body. Do I loathe my beautiful stomach now? No, I thank it every morning for being a part of me. I think about the Greek goddesses and their beautiful curves, and I see myself in this light also.

When those negative demons start talking in my mind, I acknowledge them and send them away. By addressing the negative thoughts immediately and then releasing them, I allow myself to move beyond self-loathing.

Facing the negative thoughts has changed my life. I am more confident, aware of patterns during stressful times and open and accepting of myself. This process is continual. Every day, I say positive affirmations in place of the negative thoughts.

My mother was always a bit overweight, and I watched my father insult her constantly. She was always on diets, trying to lose the weight. I look back now and realize my mother's self-confidence was damaged and weak. I believe I felt that on a spiritual level, soaking it into my self-conscious as a child and materializing it when I moved into puberty.

The media plays a huge part in this mental game of self-image. This is one of the main reasons why I stopped reading fashion magazines—they made me feel bad. I read health and spiritual magazines now. I believe as long as I keep my mind and soul healthy, my body will also stay healthy. I truly do not believe in cosmetic plastic surgery. I think it is just another mask women are fooled into wearing.

We must accept ourselves the way we are and recognize the beauty and uniqueness in each woman instead of trying to look like someone or something else.

I hug myself every day. I walk slower and feel the wonderful ground under my feet. I breathe the air and feel it caress my beautiful face. And I look into my tranquil eyes every morning and say *I love you.*

To every woman out there: May the light shine bright upon your path.

—Marcella, 29

Broken Spirit

Mostly I have loathed my looks and waistline, which was always big to me. In my youth, I envied the girls who had waists that "went in." I wasn't even overweight, but I had a hard, washboard tummy I hated (when I wished I'd appreciated it!). Years of rugby and working out with my brothers gave me six-pack abs, which was considered manly growing up. I hated every bit of it. So it started when I was fifteen. I was a rugby team captain, and pretty damn good—one of the best players on the squad—but I was also teased and bullied.

Almost every single day, I avoided looking in the mirror when putting on my clothes. I wore clothes bigger than my actual size. I tried eating more and began to skip training because no one wanted to date the "he-woman." It was a constant battle against myself. Even though working out made me feel better, the results made me hate myself.

Fast forward to when I had my second child, I gained a lot of weight, and my stomach became huge. When I first gained the weight, I didn't try to fix it, I just hated myself for it. And I regretted my feelings, which made me hate myself even more, if that makes sense.

If I could get back to being in shape, I honestly don't know how I would feel. I have always disliked my appearance. I have often said to myself, *If only I was thinner, if only I had a skinny waist or a flat tummy…* and now I'm saying, *If only I was fit, muscular….* Even if I fix this current state, I don't know if that will be the end of my self-hatred.

My upbringing was complicated. I was adopted when I was eight, and my sister never truly accepted me. I know because she reminded me every day. Because of her own insecurities, she pointed out my shortcomings when all I wanted was her love. She was the popular, beautiful one who dated everyone and the one everyone wanted. I was the tomboy sister with the athletic build and only a few friends. In addition, I was Muslim and Muslim girls must be *ladylike*, or so I thought. I had a loving mother who cared about raising good children. She supported me when I played sports just as she supported her other children in their endeavors. But parents can't protect you from everything. She couldn't protect me from the constant teasing or cruelty, the writing of "he-woman" on my locker in public school or the hiding of my gym clothes in the boys' bathroom. Some girls jumped me in the bathroom once, pulled off my hijab and cut my hair. It was overwhelming, and I'm sure contributed to how I felt about myself.

I believe the desire for acceptance broke my spirit. I realized this years later after I gained weight.

I think other women have learned to love themselves. For me, that part has taken longer. I used to feel alone, but now I am picky about whom I surround myself with. I remember reading a quote by Eleanor Roosevelt that's always stayed with me: "No one can make you feel inferior without your consent."

As silly as "we should all accept ourselves the way we are" sounds, it's almost like a bell rings in my head, and I believe in that statement. But it's a constant battle with my inner demons. As of today, I am happy with myself, but everyday I have to exercise reassurance.

One of the biggest turning points in my self-loathing—the moment I realized I needed to change the way I felt about myself—was revealed through my youngest daughter, Zoe. I was verbal about my weight in my daughter's younger years. When I was approached by my daughter's teacher, who told me she was worried about Zoe's eating habits, I paid more attention. At first, I thought it was an appetite thing, but then I noticed my daughter was skipping meals and once when I was cleaning, I found moldy lunches, which must have been weeks old, that she'd hidden in her room. My daughter physically changed before my eyes, and I could see her ribs. I cried when I asked her why she didn't eat and she said, "Because I'm so fat, Mom." It hurt me deeply because I knew she'd gotten this from me. *My hateful verbal comments caused her, at the age of eight, to starve herself or think she, too, was fat.* When I stopped putting myself down and started loving myself, my daughter followed in my footsteps—thankfully. Now she finishes her meals (and sometimes mine). Children pick up on more than we know.

To show myself love, I like to wake up and immediately think of things for which I am grateful. I love being a strong person. When I set goals, I achieve them. If I want something, I will get it—it has always been this way and that makes me happy. I also look at my health from a different perspective. Instead of focusing on my health and fitness as a vehicle to look a certain way, I ask myself, "What do I need to do to perform this way?" It's easier for me to focus on improving my performance rather than changing my looks. How my looks and body respond to this way of training and eating is a side effect.

—Ari, 36

Love, Hate and Understanding

I have always had a love/hate relationship with my body. I have struggled with weight issues most of my life and am also considered petite. *Being short and heavy do not go together easily in our society.*

I spent many years self-loathing. I'm not sure I did much to fix my physical appearance—mostly, I was just in denial. If full-length mirrors made me look fat or revealed my true size, then I only looked in the bathroom mirror. If I didn't like what I saw there, then I avoided mirrors altogether. Shopping for clothes depressed me, so I didn't do it often. I also avoided experiences that involved a connection to my body as a way to avoid having to deal with it (touch, closeness, physical activity, etc.)

My struggles over my self-appearance began at an early age—around ten—about the time that boy/girl relationships become part of your life. It's also when you begin to realize how your body is changing and judge your body in relationship to everyone else's.

Although my family eventually became close and included plenty of loving touch, there were many times during my early years this was not always stressed. They never verbalized that my appearance was acceptable or even beautiful. Instead, my weight remained a constant topic of family discussions as well as being told I was not athletic *(so why try?)*.

I always took the role of peacemaker in my family. I unconsciously felt I needed to be the best I could be to keep the family peace. I also had an older sister who was thin and I saw the amount of attention she received for this. Every role model seemed thin and beautiful. I began to feel "less than" because I was not. I started equating love to the physical qualities that attract people and not the internal qualities that sustain a relationship.

I used to think other women had it made because they didn't need to fix themselves and wonder why I was so different. I now know everyone has doubts and issues with their appearance and level of self-comfort. *I haven't met a woman yet who wouldn't change something about herself.*

Right now, my focus has been learning to live in the moment and not dwell on the past. I try to make time for a quiet moment by myself. I touch others and allow myself to be touched more, both emotionally and physically. I spend time with my son and marvel in his unbiased and awestruck view of the world.

My mindset has completely changed. I know I need to lose weight for health reasons. If the weight was gone, I would feel better physically (have more energy and stamina and be more comfortable in clothes), but I no longer feel the need to do this for anyone but myself. *I finally love and accept myself for who I am.* Any alterations now will just be icing on the cake.

I have struggled with many of the same issues as other women. It was not until my father died two years ago, and I lost a source of strength and unconditional love, that I began to actually put thought to these challenges in my life. Since then, I have begun a journey to allow me to appreciate each day for what it brings and not dwell on the past.

I also made a decision to enroll in school to study massage therapy. This single thing has probably done more than anything else in terms of coming to appreciate my body as well as bodies in general. I see their variety of shapes and sizes and understand we are all different and beautiful in our own ways.

Being able to practice a therapeutic, respectful touch with many people and experience this on my own body has reconnected me with my body and what is happening both within and outside. As I learn more about how we are all constructed and the possibilities for touching the physical, emotional and spiritual body of others, it strengthens my belief in myself.

I am at peace with who I am and how I am.

—Sharon, 39

Hopeless

I have disliked the structure of my legs since I was about thirteen. They have always been fat on the top half and straight up and down on the bottom half. I feel they lack any definition and always wished I was tall (I am five-foot-seven) with long sleek legs. I have never known how to style my hair. I usually just wear it in a ponytail. I look at other women's hair a lot and wish it were mine. *If I could have long thin legs and beautifully styled hair, I would feel much more confident and productive in life.*

I don't spend a lot of time hating my appearance. Whenever I think of it or see my reflection, I push it out of my mind. Basically, I avoid it. I do work on it by spending time at the gym, but this, too, feels hopeless most of the time.

I was raised in a strict but loving home, part of a large, busy religious family. As the youngest of four, I often felt sheltered by the rules of our religion and also brushed to the side with all of the activity going on in our house. The church we belonged to included snotty older girls who made me feel a person's appearance was more important than what was inside. I also felt separate from girls at school. Because of my family's religion, I was not allowed to hang out with them, so I wanted to hide all of the time. This says volumes about how I carried myself.

After seven years of marriage, my husband thinks I am overweight (which I am at 185 pounds) and mentions it to me in arguments. He's even gone so far as to say he's not turned on by me, and when he gets mad at me for little things, he is really mad I am overweight. I know he is embarrassed by me when we are in public or he has to introduce me to co-workers or other people he knows.

I feel jealous of women who do not have a weight problem or other problems with their outward physical appearance, but I don't feel alone. I know other women think and feel the same way I do.

I cannot accept or be content with the idea that we should all accept ourselves the way we are rather than trying to become something else. However, to show myself love, I could think positively and not allow negative thoughts to enter my mind. When they do, I need to shove them away.

Overall, I feel cheated my genes are not perfect while other women are born with perfect bodies and metabolisms. I believe the battle of my appearance is hopeless because it's not possible for me to change my body structurally. *I will always hate my body's structure.* I might be able to do something about my weight if I starve or deprive myself, which is something I will struggle with for the rest of my life. It's cruel I might have a daughter someday who will inherit the same genetic body structure, and make her dislike herself the same way I have.

—Holly, 33

Young Slave

I loathe my weight. Sometimes I spend a lot of time thinking about it, but when I find myself going the route of self-loathing, I usually write in my journal about how I can fix it, or I just start working out. I started to really notice that I didn't like my weight when I was about eleven. It wasn't that big a deal, but by thirteen, it was very hard on me and weighed on my mind often. It also paired with other insecurities about myself as a person and my personality, which I resolved almost completely about a year and a half ago.

When I was little, my Dad felt he could make up for other inadequacies in his fathering if he made sure I had all the food I could eat. Then I would be happy. Thankfully, this did not last for more than a year. During that time, he would feed me McDonald's hamburgers all the time, which is why I no longer eat them.

Being a bit of a shy person, I feel like if I didn't have my weight in the way, I might be more able to fix the things I don't like about my life. That said, if I could fix my weight problem, I don't think how I feel about myself would change, but maybe other people would see me differently. I would then have no excuse for not being as satisfied with my life in terms of friends and guys—which would be a new feeling—yet I also believe I'm quite satisfied with my life. I wouldn't want anyone's feelings for me to change according to my weight or appearance. Many of my friends feel the same way, meaning hate something about themselves, some who have no obvious reasons for feeling so.

To show myself love, I could make realistic fitness goals and to do things that make me feel good about myself often, such as write, draw, dance, act and sing. The last thing I'll share is a quote I like: "Nemo liberi est qui corpori servit*" which means "No one is free who is a slave to their body."

—Jillian, 15

*Attribution: Lucius Annaeus Seneca (often known simply as Seneca, or Seneca the Younger).

Finding Self-Worth

Physically, I dislike my teeth, wide thighs, small breasts and stretch marks. These feelings began around age fifteen. In the past, I did not have control over my reproductivity and was dependent on men for a false sense of self-worth and self-esteem. The more male attention I received, the better I felt about myself.

My struggling self-esteem greatly contributes to my feelings and I believe my upbringing contributed to my sense of self. My father abandoned my mother and me when I was five. My mother is a perfectionist and very superficial. I also think the media and social/cultural expectations of what a woman is supposed to look and be like contributed to my self-loathing.

I used to devote quite a bit of time to thinking about my imperfections, however, I am slowly beginning to accept that I am who I am. I have taken control of my reproductivity and found self-worth as I discovered who I am. Going back to college and making better choices helped me to feel better about myself. I still think I would enjoy my looks more if I could fix my teeth, breasts and thighs.

I realize almost every woman struggles with these or similar issues, but I agree we should accept ourselves for who we are and finally feel comfortable in our own skin. I would love to see a wider social acceptance of all body and female types. As women, we need to demand this.

To show myself love today, I can use positive affirmations and tell myself I am perfect and okay just as I am.

—Tesa, 26

Crunch Time

Loathe is really a strong word, but I have always somewhat detested numerous parts about my physical appearance. From my clearly "Jewish nose," to my small boobs, to my unshapely thighs, to especially my unsightly stomach, I seem to focus a little bit on a lot of things.

If I had to choose, my abs—or lack, thereof—have been the greatest point of self-loathing. After seeing the perfectly chiseled abs on every model in summer magazine issues, I could never stand the fact I didn't have them. A ballet dancer since age two, I considered a professional career but decided to go to college, a decision I'm still unsure about. Nearly every one of my ballet teachers told me my abs were not strong enough and I needed to work on them. Such frustration! They're never flat or strong enough. *No matter how many crunches I do, it's never enough to get those abs I want.*

I started hating myself in early high school. It was that point when my friends and I were changing and growing, a little past those horrible stages of puberty. Everyone found something they hated about themselves. Several of my best friends hated their stomachs, which I think made me look a bit more closely at mine. It just wouldn't have been right for me to like my stomach if they didn't like theirs! I used to self-loathe a lot more than I do now and became eating disordered for a while in high school, which involved a near-depressive state as well. I was a mess.

Ballet certainly played a factor in contributing to my self-loathing. Nobody ever told me I was too large or needed to lose weight, but looking in the mirror at oneself in skintight fabric for hours a day makes it inevitable for someone to focus on their physical appearance. Being surrounded by other practically perfect bodies (long and skinny legs, perfect shapes) provided an atmosphere that forced me to consider my own appearance. When my eating disorders first began, I lost a few pounds and got thin, but not unreasonably so for a ballet dancer. In all honesty, I looked better and more like a dancer. My teacher noticed I lost weight and complimented me but also told me not to lose any more. While he intended to warn me, the only comment I remembered was how the lost weight looked good. I figured losing more would make me look even better, and the downward spiral continued. Another factor: competition! My beautiful, social, talkative, wonderful friends all seem to have the looks and personalities I want. I simply get jealous if I can't be as wonderful as them.

I used to do crunches all the time, but I have somewhat overcome this obsession and now only sporadically do these exercises, which of course, has led to a much less-defined stomach than when I was obsessive—such an unfair tradeoff.

If I could resolve this, I'd feel more confident in myself. When I had decent abs, I was proud of them. I carried myself with confidence. But then again, I'm sure I would find more flaws to focus on. *Every girl I know—even the ones who are the most beautiful, intelligent and nice—seems to find something inherently flawed about herself.* No matter how seemingly perfect they appear to be, they will find something wrong with themselves.

I completely agree we should accept ourselves the way we are rather than trying to become something else. I just wish all of us could truly accept this viewpoint and actually act on it.

To show myself love rather than participate in self-loathing, in all honesty, I can't think of anything I wouldn't regret later. I would say eat a bowl of ice cream every day, but then I'd just get fat. I want so much to be able to completely accept myself the way I am. But even when I tell myself I'm beautiful and don't need to change, I have this morsel of doubt in my mind. I still look at girls and wish I could have their perfect figures. I still do crunches every couple of days. I still force myself to go to the gym. I still make my sister fatty dishes to eat when I see she's getting thinner than me.

I think women, and virtually all members of society, need to take the focus off the body. Why is it such an important part of our opinions of people? Why have we set before us an ideal body image? *People should focus on experiencing and loving life, not wasting time trying to change the way they were made.* A complete societal change needs to take place in order to take the emphasis off of the physical image. If I have a daughter, I think I'll have her live in a cave so she doesn't have to deal with the self-doubt our society breeds (I'm just kidding, but it's a thought!).

My personal goal is to decrease the amount of time I spend thinking about the way I look. I don't want my image to cross my mind any more than absolutely necessary. I don't want it to even be a second thought, so that I can focus on the things that really do matter.

—Becky, 18

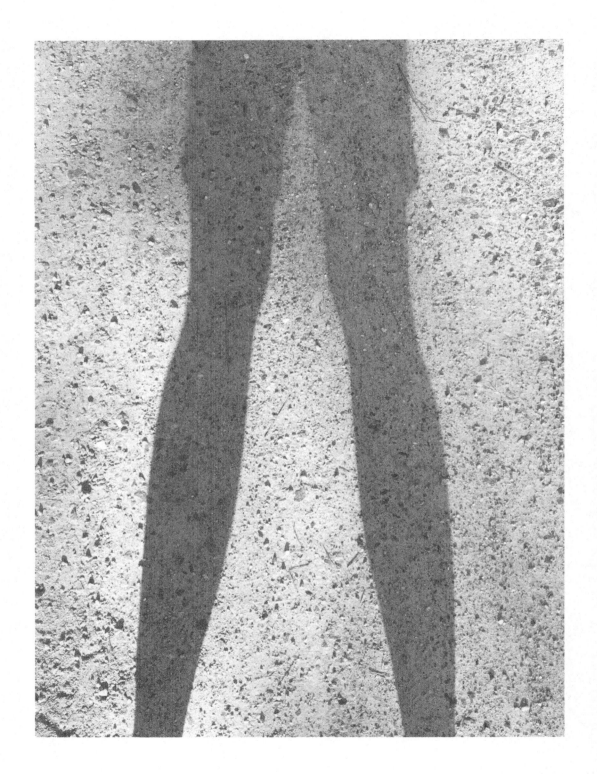

My Body Is Not Who I Am

I have always been big. Not chubby or the dreaded *fat* word, but bigger than anyone in my family or classes. My dad used to call me "Amazon." What a label that was!

I've spent so much time talking about how much I don't like my body. It's worse now that I've had two children, and according to the doctor's body mass index chart, I am clinically obese. My husband finally told me how much of a turn-off my self-destructive talk is and clarified he loves me for me and not my body. You know what's bizarre? My next thought after he said that was... *Well, that's obvious, why else would he stay with me?* How awful!

I did lose thirty pounds once. It didn't matter. I felt proud for a while and then realized I couldn't keep taking the Ephedra because I learned it might cause my heart to stop without notice. I was back to square one. The miracle I thought I'd found might actually kill me. I wasn't willing to pay that price. So, I suppose self-loathing is the lesser of two evils.

I probably started having these thoughts about myself in high school. It seemed everyone else was thin and beautiful. I didn't eat for a month once when I was sixteen. I lost twenty-five pounds and everyone, even my coaches and teachers, told me how great I looked. Thank God that made me mad. I was angry because I knew people who never ate, and they were killing themselves. Even then, I realized how terrible and dangerous it could be to encourage weight loss in teens. In their defense, maybe they thought I did it the right way.

I guess I've always had glimpses of light where I know God loves me and my family loves me, and that's all that matters. I have since learned *I must also love me* to truly be healthy. Another thing—I remember an uncle mentioning my curves when I started to develop. This was the beginning of the realization that men noticed my physical attributes and my wanting to please them.

I am a pleaser. The book, *The 5 Love Languages* by Gary Chapman*, explains how we all have a certain way we express love and want to be loved back. I believe my love language is "words of encouragement." This makes sense because I have constantly strived for approval, mostly from my father. My mother died of cancer when I was thirteen. I was the oldest girl and took on the motherly role. Nothing I ever did seemed good enough for Dad. Appearance was everything. *I learned very quickly to just look pretty and it would make everything all right.*

Some years ago when Christopher Reeve gave his first interview to Barbara Walters after his accident, I was riveted to my TV screen. He said something so profound, it brings tears to my eyes every time I think about it: *"I am okay because my body is not who I am."* That was such a revelation to me! My faith tells me the same, but for some reason, I'd never thought of it that way. What a relief! Even though I lapse into familiar self-loathing territory, I remember I am a soul...loved and capable of so much love. My body is not who I am! Praise God for that! Anyway, it's all relative. My skinny friends hate their bodies, too.

Hear, hear to accepting ourselves just the way we are. I think that idea is brilliant! But I know I feel better when I look better. I am not sure how to explain that one except since having children, I have become more focused on health instead of being a size six, and so the definition of looking better has changed a bit for me.

To show myself love today, I choose to use words of affirmation. In different seasons of my life, I have actually written affirmations to learn to talk *nicely* to myself. For example: I am a great mother. I adore growing and learning with my children. Today I am enough! I have character and value just the way I am.

—Cathy, 33

*The five ways to express and experience love that Gary Chapman calls "love languages" are receiving gifts, quality time, words of affirmation, acts of service and physical touch.

Erase It

For the past few years, I have hated my cellulite, specifically on my thighs, and my coarse, curly hair. Now that I have a fifteen-month-old baby, I don't have a lot of time for self-loathing, but I would feel better about myself if I could lose weight, get rid of the cellulite on my thighs and erase my scar from my C-section.

I believe I feel this way as a child of divorce, with a neat-freak mother for whom I could never do anything right. My father was just never around much. I also am divorced and tend to be in emotionally and physically abusive relationships. *I know I deserve better, but I don't know how to get out of them.*

I know I'm not alone in how I feel. I see this every day of my life. Many of my female friends and family members are going through the same thing. I understand I should be self-accepting, but it's hard to do when those close to me are having plastic surgery and breast implants I can't afford.

To change how I feel and show myself love, I can try to look in the mirror, smile and feel comfortable without makeup.

—Lori, 33

Early Bloomer

I never liked my body as a young woman. Being well-developed by age twelve, I was uncomfortable. At home, my father never paid attention to me. I was lost in the midst of my brother's and dad's chauvinistic outlook about women. I tried so hard to be "one of the guys"—and I succeeded for a while. Because I was an early bloomer, I was heavier and curvier sooner than my friends. When I was in sixth grade, the school decided we had to play flag football instead of tackle at recess. I know it was because a few of us girls were becoming young women and it wasn't *appropriate* for the boys to be tackling us. *I felt betrayed by my body.* I didn't like that I was a girl.

In fourth grade, I remember being weighed in gym class and the teacher reading all of our weights out loud. I was at the upper end but knew it was better to be one of the cute *little* girls. I think this sort of thinking also sets women up to hate one another, instead of having strength of friendship.

Because I never received unconditional love from my parents, I believed and accepted the world's idea of beauty. As I got older, I never liked my body, but learned that boys and men did. I always wanted to be thinner. There probably was a brief time when I felt attractive enough, but that was because I was attractive to men, not because I liked myself. I spent lots of money and time to prop up that feeling—as well as jumping in and out of bed with different men.

I don't spend a lot of time self-loathing anymore. Just recently, I've been working with a counselor. I am a Christ follower, finding the unconditional love missing my whole life. *What I know is I am perfectly and uniquely made and God loves me now at sixty pounds overweight as much as He did when I was at my perfect weight.* The reality is I don't have the power to change my weight, but He has the power to move in me.

That said, there are many, many days I look at others and wish I were thinner, in better physical shape or had nicer clothes to wear. Part of it is I don't feel I deserve to spend the time on myself. It's hard to stop taking care of everyone and everything else to focus on me.

Now that I'm almost forty, I feel more comfortable with my imperfections. I would like to be healthier, not to impress others but because it feels better. I want to be able to run with my kids, not sit on the sidelines and watch them. I want to look better, have new clothes and look put together because it makes me feel happier and it's fun, not to attract men, which was my previous barometer of whether I was *worthy* or not. Everyone wants to be desired and looked at with respect. Both of those things don't come by being in perfect physical shape or having the right "look."

I'm convinced we go through such self-loathing because we were never given unconditional love. Parents missed the boat in the last generation, and we're still doing it today. It means letting yourself off the hook. It means having more energy and a comfortableness with yourself. I haven't changed anything physical, but my heart has changed. My outlook has changed. I'm not so focused on myself. My weight has no impact on my success as a person. I can still love my children and husband and do well at what I do. Others don't look at me in disgust as I once thought they did because I'm heavier than I'd like.

I wish it was as simple as just getting rid of a part of me. It's harder to change our emotional states. It's hard to go back to my childhood and uncover the lies I learned: 1) girls don't matter, 2) they must always look good or there is no worth, and 3) my physical state is more important than the state of my heart. *Those lies colored my entire life.* And while my mother didn't actively push these things, she didn't do anything to protect me from learning them. Her actions of always being made-up before leaving the house and being unhappy with herself taught me that was how to be a woman.

I also believe there is an elusive "perfect woman" or "perfect man" out there in the media that comes to live in our psyche. Coupled with bad parenting and conditional love, we accept those external influences as truth.

I don't know many women who are comfortable with themselves. The few I really respect are the friends who have made some changes in their lives. They've done it because they wanted to feel better about themselves, not because they were bowing to an external force. I don't think I'm alone in thinking this way. I wonder how much energy some women put into looking good and what motivation they have. Are they spending lots of time preparing themselves every day and feeling scared not to be seen without makeup on or in perfect clothes? I wonder if they feel like they're nothing without those things.

Each day to show myself love, I can bask in the love that Jesus Christ has for me. Without the acceptance He is the true north, I get lost quickly in the attacks of the world around me about how I should look. I find nothing wrong with my aging, for example. I don't want to dye my hair when the gray comes in. I don't want to spend thousands of dollars on cosmetic surgery to stay young. It's like trying to have perpetual spring and that isn't natural. I also can surround myself with people who are true friends, not ones who like me for how I look.

—Juli, 39

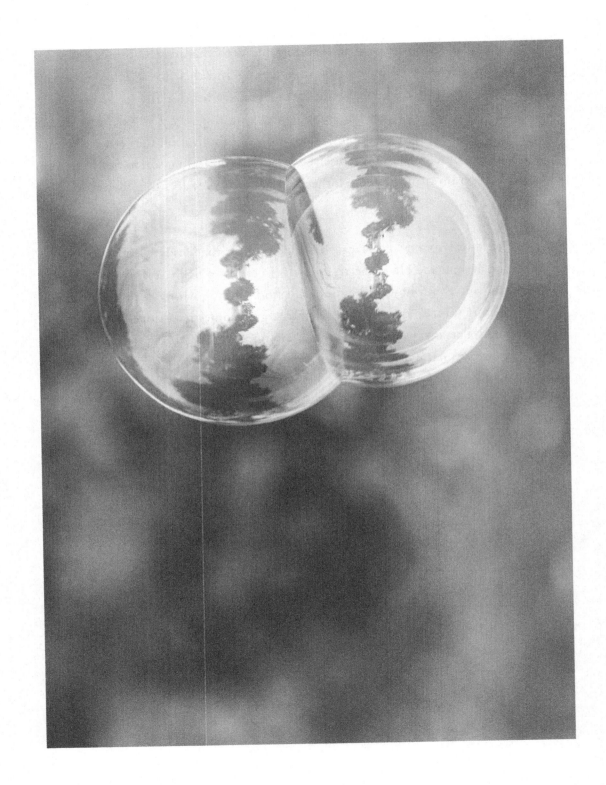

Bubble Butt

There are body parts which I have been especially aware as being different than those of *normal women*. These parts are my hips, thighs and ass. They are especially large in comparison with the rest of my body and have been since I was about seven, when I wore a miniskirt on the first day of second grade and the female teacher made a comment to my mom about what a "bubble butt" I had for a young girl. I think she said I had the body of a woman already or something to that effect.

I spend a huge amount of time trying to fix this "problem" by going to the gym and eating mostly healthy foods. I am a bit opposed to saying that I loathe these parts of my body, but I certainly spend a lot of time looking in the mirror and wishing these parts were different, meaning smaller and more toned.

I definitely know if these aspects of my body were *fixed*, I would be a lot less self-conscious, especially about my ass. I am conscious about it at every point during the day, and resolving it would free up some of the space in my brain to use for more productive things.

My upbringing definitely contributed to my feelings. My mom was always overweight and on a diet, so this has been a part of my lifestyle as long as I can remember. My aunt is the one who really made me self-conscious about my body and helped shape the way I see myself today. Every time I went to her house, she said, "You would be so beautiful if you weren't fat." She wouldn't let me have soda or food that she would eat in front of me, and she always made me go for hikes when I visited. Her comments really stuck with me after hearing them for a decade of my childhood. Needless to say, I don't speak to her today.

My insecurity also contributes. I constantly compare my body to other women's bodies, whether they are in the media or at school, and never feel I completely measure up in the gorgeous body arena. I do have a beautiful face and my body isn't *that bad,* but I find myself thinking, *Why would God waste such a beautiful body on someone with such an ugly face? Why can't I have that body? Then I would be perfect.*

Women with perfect bodies have it made. Because I know how aware I am of my body at all times, I think, "I bet you haven't worried about your body or the way your ass looks all day long. That makes you lucky." I definitely don't feel alone in thinking the way I do about my body. There are many women out there in worse shape than I am. And sometimes I'm thankful for my body because I see women I believe would give anything to be my size, even though I'm a little overweight.

Accepting ourselves the way we are, rather than trying to become something else, is an uplifting thought. By accepting our bodies the way they are, which I am actively trying to do, we are empowering ourselves. I should try to look in the mirror and see my hips and ass as something that makes me special. When I see all these skinny girls, I realize my ass makes me special while the skinny girls are a dime a dozen.

—Kim, 22

Inescapable

I've always been obsessive when it comes to my weight and appearance. While in high school, I ran cross-country and track and was quite thin at five-foot-two and roughly ninety-five pounds. I stopped running due to work and school schedules when I was seventeen and rapidly began gaining weight, reaching one hundred and forty pounds. I had a boyfriend who didn't seem to mind, plus full-time college and work schedules to deal with, so I didn't really notice it until I was about twenty-one. By then, I had dropped out of college, broken up with my boyfriend of seven years and was finally living alone. When I realized I was overeating, I quickly changed to eating one meal consisting of four hundred calories a day, then moved on to obsessive exercising—Tae Bo for an hour, then later in the day, I would run six miles or so.

After a few months, my body morphed into what I *thought* would make me feel happy, complete and confident again. I weighed one hundred and ten pounds and looked great! But then I got married at twenty-four, divorced eight months later due to his infidelities, and stopped exercising altogether due to depression.

Now at age twenty-six, I've found myself in the same cycle...*again*. I recently started dating a longtime friend, who is wonderful, and have gone back to school, but I find myself thinking all of the horrible thoughts I once did. I weigh one hundred and thirty pounds—which isn't bad—but when I look at myself, I see someone completely different than before. I don't even look like the same person of two years ago.

I know I wasn't happy when I was thin. It's the image of self-confidence—of looking healthy, happy and fun—that still distorts and sabotages me. *At times, I believe I will never be happy with myself, but I should at least physically appear like I am.*

Do I spend a lot of time self-loathing, trying to fix something I hate, or both? *Yes, practically twenty-four hours a day.* I think about it constantly, while dressing and getting ready for classes or work, while eating (I think people are looking at me and thinking I shouldn't be eating at all), while working (I'm a waitress and constantly feel awkward about my apron being too tight, causing my midsection to bulge or my arms to show, etc.). I dream about people leaving me or not wanting to have sex with me because I'm too heavy. I spend a lot of time trying to fix myself. I've been in therapy for about three years now. I began seeing a nutritionist and changed my diet. I see a personal trainer and work out in my college gym.

I don't feel fixing my self-image comes directly from my body image, at least it didn't before. I was always an awkward child with my kinky, curly hair and just seemed different, but I really started obsessing about myself when I hit twenty-one. My father was a terrific dad, but he was an alcoholic who regularly abused my mother. In turn, she verbally and physically abused me because she perceived he loved me more than her. Through therapy, I've learned my opinion was never accounted for, never mattered, and it has therefore, manifested in and controlled my adult life. When my parents were together, I thought they fought about my behavior, grades or messy room. I blamed myself for their divorce. When my father remarried, he stopped drinking, causing me to wonder if *I* was the reason he drank so heavily, or if he couldn't stand to be with us sober. I now understand that wasn't the case at all, but the feelings remain. When my dad left, I was twelve and my mother was never home to take care of my brother (who was only two) and me. I felt abandoned, as if no one cared about us. All of this contributed to where I am now.

I don't believe I'm alone in how I feel or my obsession. Most of my friends have similar problems with self-image, body image and self-esteem, even the gorgeous ones! A part of me gets angry I've spent so much valuable time trying to change myself, all the while knowing the physical change isn't what is or was necessary. *Part of me feels relieved about the idea of accepting ourselves as we are, as if that's what I've been waiting to hear all along.*

I've purchased a day planner with daily exercises, meditations and affirmations geared toward self-healing. Sometimes I love them and they make me feel great. Sometimes I hate them and simply tolerate them with hopes of recovering. I need to get rid of, and am working on getting rid of, negative thoughts and phrases that occur all of the time without a second thought.

—Lesan, 26

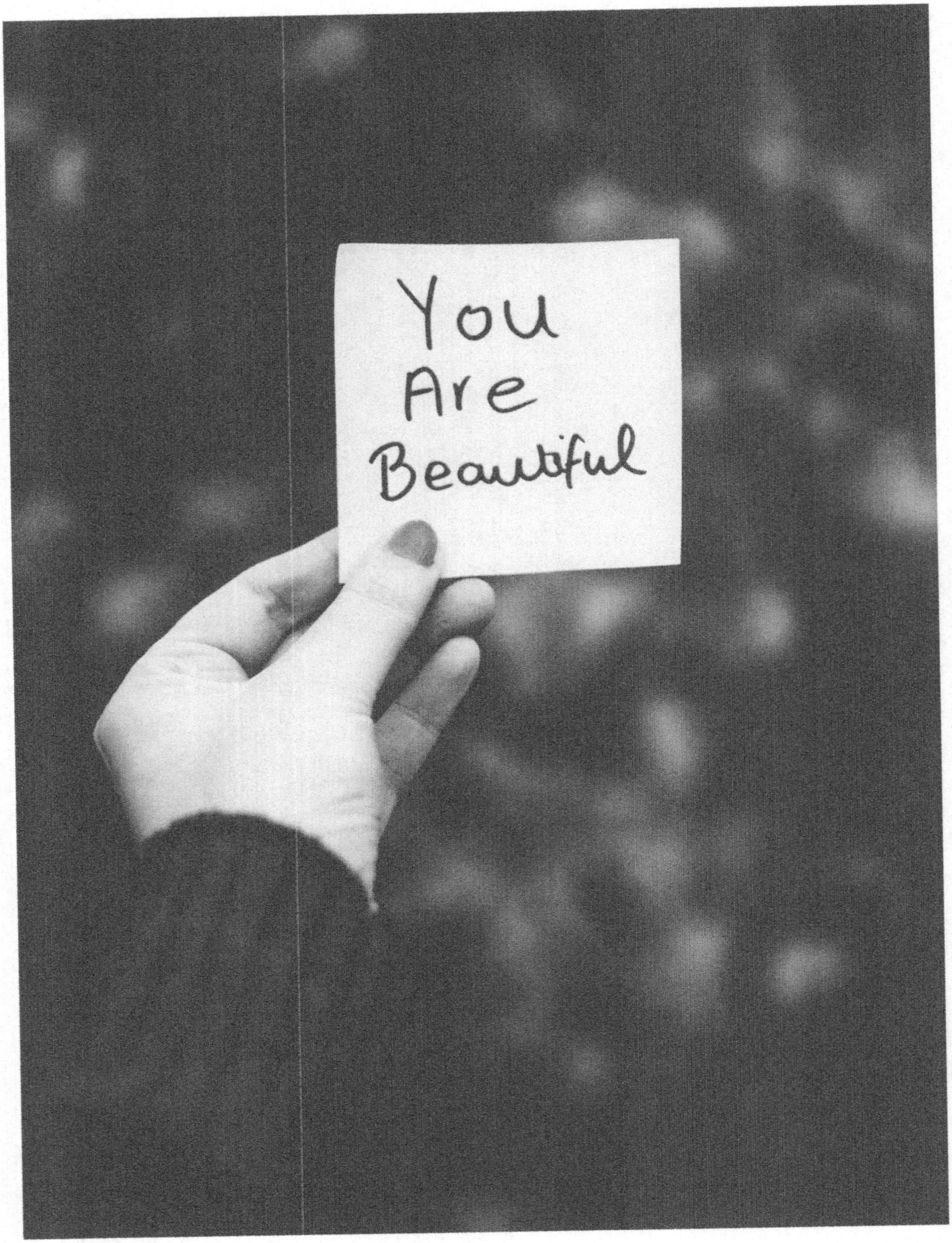
You
Are
Beautiful

Working It Out

I used to hate my big butt and smaller breasts, and I hate my weight now because it affects my physical well-being, but I don't spend much time self-loathing now. For a long time after I became obese, I used to think being thin again would make me more loveable—this was before I started loving myself the way I am.

In my younger years, I always wondered what was wrong with me. I hated this part of myself, and didn't like the rest much, either, until about five years ago. I used to want a bigger bust like my grandmother, maybe because she loved me so much and I was fond of her. I realize now I am like her on the inside, which is the important part.

My upbringing definitely contributed to my way of thinking. Alcoholism ran in my family. Both of my parents were critical and abusive. My mother didn't like or love me, and that hasn't changed. My dad loved me—and is now able to say and show it—but out of fear of losing his relationship with my mother, he often didn't express it. After their divorce, he met someone who truly loved him and our relationship evolved. As an adult, until I asked my dad to stop likening me to the worst traits of my mother, *I constantly questioned my likeability and loveability.* Navigating all of that wasn't the only thing to change my attitude toward myself, but it did help.

Other contributing factors? Society in general—specifically men—judges women by their outsides first. It happens in the job market, schools and most groups in which women take part. *Men have a network that accepts them automatically, while women have to prove themselves over and over and over.*

I believe all women, regardless of their outer appearance, have a need to *fix* themselves. That is, until they realize (through counseling, reading, support from other women who have been there, etc.) they are fine—even wonderful—just the way they are and will be, whether they decide to change anything about themselves.

In my twenties and thirties, I didn't like other women much. I was thin, shapely and didn't care if they liked me because their men did, and I was okay with me. I didn't like myself at all. Today, I am closer to women than men. I've found the sisterhood of women—one where we help each other grow and the love that develops among us—to be so beautiful! I love being a woman with its many facets, and wish all women would grow to this point and beyond.

I have worked on myself in great depth, grown a great deal and will continue to do so. I no longer wonder, *What's wrong with me?* My goal for today is striving for health in all areas.

There are several ways I practice self-love rather than self-loathing, including looking in the mirror and telling myself I am beautiful inside and out, being kind to myself in little ways (e.g., not getting too tired or lonely, having a bubble bath, taking a walk and enjoying nature) and beginning my day with prayer and meditation to foster the connection to my spiritual being and higher power.

I wish all women would encourage and accept each other for where we are in our path of growth today. This is an ideal, as no one is always able to be there for another, but I like to try.

—Nancy, 55

Measuring Up

In college, I gained weight and added about ten pounds each decade thereafter. I spent a lot of time self-loathing and trying to fix my weight problem, but *did more hating than fixing*. I have lost the forty pounds I accumulated since high school. Although I feel much better, I found new things to loathe, such as in the areas of wealth and education and the levels I've reached—or rather, *not reached*.

I believe my peers and the media's image of women caused my loathing. I think women who don't have to work at fixing their problems often don't admit they are working desperately at it—either through exercise, diet, expensive spa treatments or home remedies.

Accepting ourselves the way we are rather than trying to become something else is an ultra-feminist ideal—not in a negative way—but one that understands women and our hidden beauty.

I could show myself love by truly not taking stock in what other people think of me or caring whether they judge me if I choose to wear sweats instead of a matching outfit, go without any makeup or not style my hair.

—Miriam, 38

Fugazi

I loathe my overall body image. *I try my best to be perfect and in my mind, skinny is perfect.* I love it when my clothes are loose. If I had to pinpoint one part of my body I dislike specifically, I would say my outer thighs, where I have cellulite. I work out everyday, except the one day each week I take off. I get upset if my workouts are interrupted or I can't work out on a day I planned. I base my social life around working out and tend to not make any plans during the week because it might interfere.

I don't think it would change my life if I could fix this. With my personality, I would move on to another "something" I would like to fix. I'm always striving to be better, look better, make more money and put on a happy face.

I started hating my body as a whole when I was eight years old. I moved to different parts of my body throughout my life. I used to hate my chest, but got breast implants— *so I fixed that.*

My mother put a great deal of pressure on me. I played sports and had talent. The better I played, the more pressure she heaped on me. When I got a scholarship to play soccer at the U.S. Military Academy West Point, I attended. West Point, located on the bank of New York's Hudson River, put a lot of pressure on women to be thin. As I was going through my freshman year, my team leader told me not to succumb to the "Hudson Hip Disease." The *disease* was common among female cadets, known for gaining weight and subsequently, not looking good in their uniforms. As a result, I increased my workouts and went through a minor bout of an eating disorder. I just didn't eat much. I lost a great deal of weight and looked horrible. People intervened, and I got back on track pretty quickly.

Later, once I began working in an office, my mother told me I should continue exercising to avoid getting *office spread*. It's amazing how those two comments have stuck with me. My mother still frequently asks if I worked out already when she calls.

I tend to have a temper and can snap at people. I am sometimes unfriendly and worry people won't like me. I also don't take the precious time to straighten my hair, so I wear it up a lot. I know this is extremely petty, but I do pick on myself for that small detail. *Perfect women are always friendly and have great hair, right?*

I think some women choose not to fix their flaws because they accept who they are. I admire those women, but at the same time wonder if they ever strive to improve themselves. As for my thoughts about my own body and efforts to resolve flaws, I don't feel alone. I have always surrounded myself with competitive women. I am currently in the Army, surrounded by zealous and ambitious women who strive to fix or improve facets of their selves and behaviors all the time.

If I could accept myself as I am, I'd be less stressed and probably less hungry. As I grow older, I am accepting and embracing parts of me. *I hope I reach a point in my life where I can accept myself.* To be honest, I don't know how to show myself love each day rather than participate in self-loathing.

I may come across as insecure and perhaps unbalanced, but I am a confident woman who has been successful at work and at home. I married an incredible husband, who is in a high-risk career and gone seven months out of the year, which may add fuel to the fire of my search and need for perfection. Every time he goes away, I try to better myself so he will be proud of me when he returns. I spend a great deal of time by myself because of his absence. When he is home, I work out less and am more accepting of myself.

—Lynn, 29

*Fugazi is a military term that originated during the Vietnam War meaning "out of whack, fucked up, screwy."

Mixed Messages

Growing up, I hated being teased for my big nose—I was called Pinocchio—and being skinny. Many of the females among my family and friends were overweight and miserable. When I grew up, had babies and got fat, I felt like I'd finally joined the club. I looked at skinny women and then understood how my family and friends felt toward my skinny younger self. Comments then turned into, "Watch yourself, you don't want to get too big!" It was confusing. Something was wrong with me whether I was skinny or fat?

My mother is deeply in denial about self-loathing, as was my grandmother and aunt. As I grew up, to be fat was normal and to be skinny was bad.

I've had many failed attempts at losing weight and getting in shape. I had no role model to do this and no support to do it right. I had my weight issues as a teen, plus depression and alcohol abuse. I was out of control and out of touch with myself with zero self-esteem or self-worth. I had a baby at twenty-one and another at twenty-nine. My self-image went from glowing maternal "Madonna with child" to "fat and ugly" when my first child turned three and I had ballooned back to the weight I was at her birth. Thus began the cycle of unhealthy weight-loss and half-hearted exercise programs. I fit into the jeans I wore right after she was born a few months before I became pregnant with my son. After his birth, I nursed for thirteen months. The weight came off rapidly, but came right back when I began weaning. I felt lost and hopeless. My weight skyrocketed back to the weight I was at his birth when he was two. I started the cycle again—and I never fit into those jeans on my own.

I joined Gold's Gym a year ago, then I joined Healthy Inspirations, a weight-loss program at the gym. Now those jeans are way too big for me, and I'm being called "skinny" again. This time, I know it's with love that they say it. There are women at the gym whose level of fitness I'd love, but then I hear they've had this enlarged or that fixed and they're going back to make 'em even bigger! Then I lose the desire to be like them.

It's hard to find a role model for health and fitness in our society, and it's disheartening to know you can't find one at the gym, either. I stay focused on my health and fitness. I ignore the negative messages in the world and seek only that which is positive and healthy. Yet it is still tempting to get my sagging breasts and belly fixed so I will look proportioned. I'm not anxious to have surgery, but I do stand in front of the mirror and hold my breasts up and suck in my tummy to see what it might be like. It's not something I have to do to feel better about myself even though it is tempting when you see the results of surgery to fix saggy parts. It won't make me a better person, so I try to focus on accepting myself.

It has been an emotional struggle. I don't want to be perfect for my husband because I don't think I should have to. I know he'd love me to fix it all and wear a bikini, but it's my body and I won't go that far to please him with a perfect image, a dream or some picture of an ideal woman based on the images society feeds men. That said, it is a struggle and temptation not to believe that by fixing things, I will be lavished with attention and affection. And yet, I realize my husband loves me any way I am. Healthy change is good but changing to become "ideal" is unhealthy.

I used to think other women had it made because they didn't need to fix themselves. Take any Hollywood beauty, for instance, who is beautiful, young looking, sexy, funny and rich. They always seem happy, but they sacrifice privacy, intimacy, their families and sometimes freedom. The image they portray doesn't bring them happiness. So I've learned that changing my outward image doesn't change who I am on the inside.

To show myself love rather than participate in self-loathing, I reward within reason. I don't use food to make myself feel better, and I don't deprive myself thinking I will feel better. I attempt a healthy balance to achieve self-love. I give my body what it needs to be healthy and fit, and that makes me happy.

—Tami, 35

Unsettling

I loathe always seeing things in myself I want to improve. My weight was first, and I did well with that. Right now, my biggest issue is I always seem to *settle* for the wrong person in my life. I've felt this way since I was seventeen and with my now ex-husband.

I am happy being alone most of the time. Between working two jobs, taking care of my fourteen year-old son and trying to maintain friendships, I am busy. In my spare time, I try to do little things for myself, like getting my nails done, and appreciate that someone is doing something for me for a change. But then I find myself wanting to be married, having another child before I'm too old and spending the rest of my life with my soulmate. I wind up going out with the wrong guys, the kind who have most—but not everything—of what I desire in a partner. I settle for someone who meets part of the criteria, only to find out I can't stand them a few months later! They are never what I believe them to be. It's very discouraging and disappointing, yet I seem to continue doing it. This is something I greatly dislike about myself.

I spend a lot of time self-loathing and trying to fix what I hate. *I say I won't make the same mistakes, but then I do it again and spend the next few weeks or months beating myself up over it.*

I pick on myself a lot. Because I was a mom at nineteen and had to be independent, perhaps now my independence has an effect on my relationships. I never seem to be completely happy with the men I choose, but I also like to do things my way, in my time, and that is probably difficult to handle.

If I stopped settling for what is "good enough for now" and focused on the long-term, I'd probably be happy. I can't imagine how it would affect my life because it's never happened. I attempt to do the right things for myself, my son and others so I can at least sleep at night knowing I behaved in ways both right and just.

I'm sure other women have it made, but I don't know anyone who is completely happy with the life they've chosen. It's a part of growing, and part of life, to find things we want to change, or desire what we want versus what we have. I feel alone sometimes, yes. But my son and a few wonderful friends help me realize I will never be alone as long as they are in my life.

Although I think we should all accept ourselves the way we are, I also don't think it's possible to be happy with one's self all the time. There are bound to be circumstances that cause us to judge ourselves, regret past choices and beat ourselves up.

To show myself love rather than participate in self-loathing, I will continue to accept my flaws and know that as long as I am on this earth, I will be imperfect. It's finding acceptance in a partner that seems to be my big problem.

—Teresa, 34

Fine at Forty

In my late teens and early twenties, I obsessed about weight. I have a normal—therefore curvy—body, which at the time, I hated. I would fast for days at a time, and other times, would stuff myself then make myself throw up. I developed breasts early, and really hated the attention I *(they)* received. As I got into my teens, I hated the assumption I was sexually active because I had a "voluptuous" body. I think the obsession with weight had to do with trying to control my physical image so it would somehow reflect I had a brain and not just a body. Being brought up in a strict Catholic family and all the guilt associated with that certainly didn't help. Fortunately, I had positive people in my life that helped me realize this was not the way to live.

I don't spend a lot of time on this topic anymore, although I do cover the gray regularly. *At forty, I have come to accept myself the way I am.* I have no desire or energy to try and be perfect, but I also think women are expected to do it all—and also do it while living up to some media-created image of the *"perfect"* mom or wife or worker. Women are always measuring themselves up to some ideal instead of their own personal goals.

Although I have come to accept myself the way I am, I feel in the minority when I hear other women talking about dieting or wanting boob jobs. Believing your life might be better "if only" is a sad way to live. I wish all women would encourage each other to accept themselves as they are, but women tend to be so competitive and always looking for some flaw in each other that they can compare themselves to (e.g., "She is a great_____, but I have better_____.") Sad, really.

To show myself love, I take time each day to do something that makes me happy and feel good.

—Suzanne, 40

I Work Out

I've always had a muscular build. My body is what I would describe as boyish. When I was younger, I loved it, and the boys thought I was strong and could keep up. As I got older, it was less attractive. I am extremely small-chested…not even an A cup, which in my opinion, makes it worse. Yes, I have often thought about having my breasts done, not just to be a larger size but to be *a* size…a full B, actually—that would be nice.

My mother was obsessed about her weight and I remember constantly hearing, *"Does this make me look fat?"* or *"I feel frumpy"* (I guess that's somewhere between fat and lumpy). She never dieted, per se, just complained. She was not large, never overweight, just thick…but oh, never satisfied. I can remember going with her to Jazzercise every night after work. I think that's where my love for exercise began, watching her, and I would join in because I thought it was fun.

I believe my body image was molded by my mother, so I promised myself I would never talk about my weight or appearance to my kids. They see me exercise and eat healthfully, but I never use the words *diet* or *off limits*. I may say, "That is not a healthy choice for me," but I try to watch the buzzwords.

Some may think I spend a lot of time exercising. I usually work out two hours five to six days a week. I love it. It's almost an addiction in itself—there is such an energy when you walk into a busy gym. I exercise because I *love* to exercise. Today I am looking more to define my body and separate the muscles, and that is as much about watching my diet as the amount I weigh.

I believe I am realistic about what changes I can actually attain in my body outside of surgery. I am not saying I would never have surgery, but that is not a goal. I love to see my body change—watching the muscles develop is great. For me, the only enhancement would be the breasts. It would help add confidence, I would feel sexier in a suit and I guess, round off the changes I'm already making.

I have always been small-chested. Today, society focuses so much on large-chested women, but I cannot say that has affected me or caused me to feel less about myself. *There is such a push for surgery these days.* A lot of women can, and do, have surgery and still don't feel their ideal, so having it is then wasted in my opinion. My question is, where do you stop? Let's say I had the surgery and then felt like, "Well, that didn't do it," and then I believed having my stomach lipoed would finally fix it and then that doesn't do it, either...it could be never-ending. At some point we have to say, "This is me" and accept it.

Perfection is not obtainable in my opinion, but a level of satisfaction is. I can be satisfied with my body and my image, but there is always room for improvement.

Starting off each day doing something for yourself (such as exercising) is a healthy way to treat yourself. I think that's why each one of us pushes harder and keeps moving. *When we get into those thoughts of self-loathing, we need to see what is missing in ourselves.* Am I hungry, angry, lonely or tired? I mean really asking ourselves why we are saying the things we are saying. For me, it generally goes back to something else.

In a room full of women, say thirty women, twenty to twenty-five will say they don't like something about themselves. It may be their hair, weight, butt, thighs or attitude, but they will name something. *It's like we are not supposed to like ourselves.*

If a woman spends two hours a day at the gym, she is selfish, prideful, cares more about herself than others, etc. I overheard two women talking at a local fast food restaurant one day about going into a local gym they considered joining, however, they knew several women who go *daily* and spend *way* too much time there. They were so negative about how these women could do that, citing their poor kids, how they could never, and so on. So some condemn women for even going. I think we have to reach inside and decide what we want to define us. We allow others to define who we are, and that, to me, is more the question...*why do we do that?* It has taken me a long time to get to this point in my own life, but when I stop and say, "How will this define me?" that puts it in a whole new light.

—Kerrieann, 36

Painfully Large

I started developing breasts at the age of twelve and by the time I was sixteen, I was wearing a C cup. Boys would tease me in a crude, cruel way and those that didn't, clearly seemed to notice. I didn't like my thighs either, starting about the same time. They were not as big of an issue because they were easier to hide. When I was pregnant, my breasts grew larger and never got smaller. I really hated the way they looked. It was impossible to find a comfortable bra. *Over the years they became grotesque.* I wanted reduction surgery from the first time I heard about it, but my husband wouldn't hear of it.

When I finally did have the reduction surgery, it was wonderful. Even though I am a C cup now, they feel the right size, and I am pleased. No more issues with my breasts!

I started to get out of the self-loathing rut around age fifty but don't think I was really okay until I committed to my own independent life at fifty-nine.

The only thing about my upbringing that may have contributed to my self-loathing: *I was never shown, taught or encouraged to stand up for myself.* My mother had her own problems with weight and beat herself up over it. In addition to that, I lived with a verbal abuser for almost forty years.

It took a long, long time to realize that other people's lives were not as perfect as they seemed.

We should accept ourselves the way we are and not beat ourselves up. We should also be kinder to other women and strive to be much less judgmental. Spending a few minutes in reflection about one's life journey and being grateful is one way to be kinder to ourselves each day.

—Linda, 65

Weighed Down

Body image has always been an issue for me. As long as I can remember, I have been obsessed with my weight. I am obese. I think about my weight and being fat all the time. It's terrible. However, I know if I lost seventy pounds, I would be gorgeous and feel fantastic. I am also clinically depressed and my depression has gotten worse as I've aged. I see a therapist several times a month.

When I was a little girl, six or maybe seven years old, I remember my aunt and grandma were obese. My grandma had to make her own clothes because she couldn't fit into anything ready-made. They always talked about being fat. My mother was rail thin, five-foot-nine, blonde and beautiful. I was a chubby little girl as babies normally are, however, *Mama zeroed in on my weight when I was in the sixth grade and never stopped.* My sixth grade teacher sold this powdered diet shake drink. Mama and I drove to her house after school one day and bought a thirty-day supply. I drank it three times a day and was starving. There was absolutely no reason for me to be on a diet. I was already five-foot-six and a perfect weight. I had no one to tell me anything different. Oddly, the whole time Mama told me I needed to lose weight, she also called me beautiful. But I've hated the way I look and obsessed about my weight since sixth grade—and that's a long damn time.

Years ago, I would go to Weight Watchers, lose weight and then drop out. I wasn't even obese back then. I gained over seventy-five pounds when I broke my ankle, then had a hysterectomy, surgery for two hernias and a broken foot, all in the span of three years. I tried joining an early morning intense exercise group. It was exciting, and I had a good friend holding me accountable. Early morning was the only time I could go because I take care of my parents twenty-four hours a day and seven days a week, and they were asleep at this time. I went four times. I couldn't believe it, but both my parents started waking up right as I was leaving to walk out the door to exercise. I stopped going and haven't been back. I gained twenty pounds.

Not only do I have a low self-esteem, but I also have the constant criticism about my weight from my husband and at eighty-three-years-old, my mother still gives me crap about my weight. So I have two foes in my house giving me negative feedback all the time.

There was one time I got thin. My husband thought I was hot for a while, and then I think he became threatened. I don't think it would matter to him if I weighed ninety pounds—to him it wouldn't be enough and he would find something else not to like.

I attribute most of my suffering to my programming as a child by my mother but also the negative crap I receive from my husband. I am also stressed taking care of two elderly parents. Being clinically depressed doesn't help, however, that comes and goes because I do have good days. When your self-esteem as a child and adult are bashed in, it's extremely difficult to trust people. I am a survivor—this is really all I know. I don't have many women friends because it's hard for me to trust them. I was bullied by a couple of girls in high school and they really did a number on me.

I also believe people that don't have a weight problem don't have a clue the anguish people like me go through. It is agonizing.

I don't think other women are better than me nor do I feel alone in thinking the way I do about myself or my weight. I know there are more women out there who feel just the same. I've taken many chances in my life. I've had failures and successes. *It's been an interesting life, but I want more.*

I have done better with my own daughter. In fact, I vowed I'd never do to my daughter what my mother did to me. My daughter is stunningly beautiful and I've never talked to her about her weight. She's in college now, but in her younger years, when she was a little chubby, I never said a word about her weight because I knew she would grow into her body. And boy did she! Not only that, she's emerged with a terrific self-image.

It's hard for me to accept myself the way I am right now. I'm certainly not trying to be anyone else. My husband accused me of not being authentic the other night at dinner. I knew he was wrong because I wear my heart on my sleeve. I finally stood up for myself and told him he was projecting himself onto me.

It is hard for me to say what I could do to show myself love without sounding fake. The only way to answer this honestly is for me to try not to focus on my weight. This, of course, is the obvious answer. I'm really not sure how to show myself love except by getting a massage, pedicure or manicure and buying an excessive amount of books I have no time to read.

—Anne, 55

The Questions

The following are the interview questions posed to each participant. Their answers were formated into the essays seen in this volume. If you'd like to participate, please visit www.katherinecobb.com and view The Self-Loathing Project page to request the questions via email. Ongoing essays will be formatted for inclusion on the website and social media. There is also a separate self-loathing book project beginning for men, who should also visit the website for more information. If you don't want to formally participate, please consider answering these questions for your own personal growth. Some participants reported doing so was quite enlightening.

1. Is there something about yourself that you loathe or have in the past? Describe.

2. Do you spend a lot of time self-loathing, trying to fix something you hate, or both?

3. If you could get rid of or fix this part of you that you hate, what do you think would happen, how do you think you would feel, how would it change your life?

4. Can you remember when you started hating this part of yourself?

5. Is there anything about your upbringing that may have contributed to your self-loathing?

6. What other reasons or factors explain why you pick on yourself/want to be perfect/think you're not good enough?

7. Do you think other women have it made because they don't need to fix themselves? Do you feel alone in thinking the way you do about yourself?

8. How do you feel when I say you are perfect the way you are?

9. How do you feel when I say I think we should all accept ourselves the way we are rather than trying to become something else (this is not to say we should strive to remain stagnant and not grow in healthy ways, but that we should not beat ourselves up because of who we are now)?

10. What could you do each day to show yourself love rather than participate in self-loathing?

More comments and insights:

Photo Credits

Thank you to the following photographers and entities for the photos used in this book, including Englin Akyurt, Gerla Brakkee, Megan Brock, Jimmy Chan, Katherine Cobb (yup, that's me), Camila Costa, Filipe Delgado, Micky Dunn, Lisa Fotios, Ian Frome, Kat Jayne, Tasha Kamrowski, Prateek Katyal, Oleg Magni, Andrew Martin, Nelson NY, Robert Owen-Wahl, Darla Shevtsova, Francesco Ungaro, Peter W., Ginny Warner, Harald Wittmaack and Alicia Zinn.

Resources

Like the old Virginia Slims ad used to say, "We've come a long way, baby." Back when I began this project, the Internet was widely used, but social media had not yet become mainstream. Content was constantly growing and our use of the Internet constantly evolving. Needless to say, there wasn't a whole lot of information available on the topics of self-love, self-acceptance and self-loathing. That has radically changed. Simply search for the aforementioned topics, and you will have a wide variety of information at your fingertips, including websites, blog posts, podcasts, articles, books, videos, Ted Talks, social media accounts, movements and groups.

Here are some resources available based on my experience and research. Please note these are suggestions for you to consider researching, not necessarily my endorsement.

The Body Image Movement (BIM) is an internationally recognized crusade founded on the belief that your body is not an ornament, it's the vehicle to your dreams. BIM believes that everyone has the right to love and embrace their body, regardless of shape. Through educational resources, speaking events and inspiring content, the Body Image Movement, headed by founder Taryn Brumfitt, is teaching the world to love the skin they're in. Watch the video, read her book, take the class, follow her on social media and more at https://bodyimagemovement.com.

The Body Positive teaches people how to reconnect to their innate body wisdom so they can have more balanced, joyful self-care, and a relationship with their whole selves that is guided by love, forgiveness and humor. Read the book and more at https://www.thebodypositive.org.

The Self-Love Movement promotes and teaches you to put your own happiness and well-being first. https://theself-lovemovement.com

The Body Is Not an Apology is a resource to promote, demonstrate and assist in the development of a global movement toward radical self-love and body empowerment. Sign up for the email affirmations—they're terrific! https://thebodyisnotanapology.com

The Every Body is Beautiful Project strives "to help every body believe they are beautiful, as is, because we've been conditioned to believe we must change our bodies to make peace with the mirror." Read the blog, spread the word and get further help through their nonprofit, Ophelia's Place. https://theeverybodyisbeautifulproject.com

Celeste Barbour is an actor, writer and comedian. Follow her "challenge accepted" photos and videos on Instagram where she mimics models for a refreshing take on not taking yourself too seriously.

A Healthy Makeover is a celebration of food, joyful movement and nurturing of self. This blog was created by my friend, Jenn Lefebvre, who has emerged as a compelling role model for body acceptance, body positivity, health at any size and debunking common beliefs. https://ahealthymakeover.com

Books

A search yielded these and more: *Unworthy: How to Stop Hating Yourself; The Body Is Not an Apology: The Power of Radical Self-Love; Self Care: Love Yourself: How to Embrace Self-Compassion, Body Love & Self Love for Life-Changing Wellness & Self-Esteem; The Body Project: An Intimate History of American Girls; The Self-Love Experiment: Fifteen Principles for Becoming More Kind, Compassionate, and Accepting of Yourself; The Self-Love Workbook: A Life-Changing Guide to Boost Self-Esteem, Recognize Your Worth and Find Genuine Happiness; The Gifts of Imperfection: Let Go of Who You Think You're Supposed to Be and Embrace Who You Are; You Are a Badass: How to Stop Doubting Your Greatness and Start Living an Awesome Life; How To Love Yourself: Learning to Love Yourself Despite Being Unloved, Feeling Self-Hatred, and Having Self-Loathing; Health At Every Size: The Surprising Truth About Your Weight; Body Positive Power: Because Life Is Already Happening and You Don't Need Flat Abs to Live It;* and *Operation Beautiful: Transforming the Way You See Yourself One Post-It Note at a Time.*

Social Media

A search on social media yielded more than I could possibly include, so I am providing a number of hashtags you can use to search for people or organizations you want to follow or investigate (and if you can think it, there's a hashtag for it, so come up with your own list, too). Have fun exploring, and follow people you feel inspired by (it will also lead you to their websites, podcasts, blogs, resources, etc.). You never know how one little thought will help you on any given day or better, you might discover whole tribes of like-minded folks you want to join!

Body positivity and self-love: #bodypositivitymovement, #bopo, #positivebodyimage, #bodypositive, #bodypositivity, #bodylove, #everybodyisflawless, #everybodyisbeautiful, #allbodiesaregoodbodies, #selflove, #loveyourbody, #allbodiesmatter, #allbodiesarevalid, #allbodiesaregoodbodies, #comfortableinmyskin, #beinyourskin, #allbodiesarebeachbodies, #allbodiesarebeautiful, #loveyourself, #loveanybody, #selfloveclub, #selflovewarrior, #selflovebringsbeauty, #loveyourbody, #loveyourlife, #lovingyourselffirst, #selfcare, #selfcompassion, #selfcareisntselfish, #selfgrowth, #selflovematters, #journeytowellness, #bodyliberation, #bodyrespect

Confidence and empowerment: #boldbraveyou, #mindovermatter, #mindbodysoul, #confidencecrusader, #wonderwomanmentality, #strongher, #strongisthenewbeautiful, #inspiringconfidence, #womenempoweringwomen, #womenempowerwomen, #femaleempowerment

Celebrating size: #healthatanysize, #haes, #embraceyourcurves, #celebratemycurves, #celebratemysize, #beinyourskin, #curvygirl, #dopecurvyladyalert, #honourmycurves, #beautyhasnosize, #curvesarebeautiful, #fatpositive

And my personal favorite: #effyourbeautystandards

One last tip: If weight issues and/or serial dieting has been a part of your story, do yourself a favor and look into all the anti-diet stuff, too. Very empowering!

What Helped Me

Back when I started this leg of my journey, there weren't many resources, so I used a few tools that had helped my other issues and basically figured things out on the fly.

I began paying attention to the copious amount of self-loathing messages I told myself everyday. If you are like me, you don't realize the scope of these messages. Our inner voice can be such a constant, you stop hearing it. *Listen for it.* Awareness is always the first step to resolve any problem. Next, I intentionally reversed those thoughts when they came, replacing them with messages of self-love, or at the very least, calling bullshit on their voracity.

I used affirmations, talking to myself in the mirror ("Hi, gorgeous!" "You are so freaking bangin'!"), sometimes with hand gestures, like a snappy finger or two pointy fingers. Have fun with it, because it will make you laugh and remove thoughts you're an idiot for talking to yourself in the mirror. I also asked the Universe and my Higher Power (go with something greater than yourself, whatever thay may be) out loud for help moving beyond the lies to embrace my awesome self. As you can tell, I place a lot of importance on saying things out loud versus just thinking them. I think *spoken* words have power, especially to combat words we are *thinking*.

I traced some of the lies back to where they might have originated (sometimes that can help you debunk them, or at least shed light on what happened), and I finally started believing what my loving husband had been trying to help me see for years: *I am worth loving, and I am perfect as I am.*

It took time, but it worked.

Simultaneously, I worked on this project, which illuminated other issues, validated what I'd learned and illustrated the dire importance of helping women get up and out of this flagellating, disdainful mindset.

Use my tools or the plethora of resources available to you today, but do it for yourself and your healing. You don't have to live the other way, I promise. Try not to get discouraged—your self-loathing wasn't built in a day, either. Even during times that feel like one step forward, two steps back, you are making progress. Be gentle with yourself through the process. Notice when you manage to hear that inner voice, combat it or negate it altogether. Notice when you stand up to someone trying to bring you down. Notice when your behavior changes for the better. Follow people and entities online who educate and support healthy messages that speak to your needs (and on the same token, unfollow those who don't). Celebrate the wins. *Because there will be wins.*

Remind yourself you would never put up with someone spewing at you what you are allowing this inner critic to spew to you. Think of it in the third person. Heck, name it if you want. Then tell her (or him or it) to fuck off and reclaim your head space.

Remember Dorothy in the *Wizard of Oz*? She had the power to go home the whole time—she just didn't realize it. It's the same for you. You have the power—you just don't know it. Click those ruby slippers, baby!

You're awesome, you've got this, and there really is no place like home when home is a safe, kick-ass haven. And I'm talking about your brain, body and soul here. It should be your safe place, and it can be.

Cue *Somewhere Over the Rainbow...*

XXOO

About the Author

Katherine Briganti Cobb was born and raised in California's San Francisco Bay Area but has lived in the mid-Atlantic since 1989, where she has written for numerous publications. She won Best Lifestyle Columnist by the West Virginia Press Association for her award-winning editorial column, "It Is What It Is," and other writing awards from the WVPA in her career. One of her short stories was published in the 2009 Anthology of Appalachian Writers. Cobb has authored several fiction and nonfiction books. Connect with her at www.katherinecobb.com (sign up for her email list and receive a freebie), and on social media.

Made in the USA
Coppell, TX
15 December 2019

12952522R00085